Petite Patios and Intimate Garden Spaces

Petite Patios and Intimate Garden Spaces

Gisela Keil

with Christa Brand

Photography by Nik Barlo, Jr.

Schiffer Publishing Ltd

4880 Lower Valley Road, Atglen, PA 19310 USA

Picture, page 1
Nowhere is the living spirit of the Mediterranean South inspired so completely as on a patio with green plants and selected accessories from warm climes.

Picture, pages 2-3
At a desired sitting place in a garden, the colors and aromas of plants find direct contact with sense and soul.

Publication
All details have been researched conscientiously and checked with the greatest care. Yet the liability for changes or other deviations cannot be denied.

Jacket and title page photos: Nik Barlo, Jr.
Translated by Dr. Edward Force, Central Connecticut State University

Designed by "Sue"
Type set in Humanst521 BT/Humanst521 BT and ZapfHumnst Dm BT

ISBN: 0-7643-2082-3
Printed in China

Library of Congress Cataloging-in-Publication Data

Keil, Gisela.
Petite patios and intimate garden spaces / by Gisela Keil With Christa Brand ; photography by Nik Barlo, Jr.
p. cm.
ISBN 0-7643-2082-3 (pbk.)
1. Patio gardening. 2. Patios. I. Brand, Christa. II. Title.
SB473.2.K45 2004
635.9'671—dc22

2004006107

Published by Schiffer Publishing Ltd.
4880 Lower Valley Road
Atglen, PA 19310
Phone: (610) 593-1777; Fax: (610) 593-2002
E-mail: Info@schifferbooks.com

For the largest selection of fine reference books on this and related subjects, please visit our web site at
www.schifferbooks.com
We are always looking for people to write books on new and related subjects. If you have an idea for a book please contact us at the above address.

This book may be purchased from the publisher.
Include $3.95 for shipping.
Please try your bookstore first.
You may write for a free catalog.

In Europe, Schiffer books are distributed by
Bushwood Books
6 Marksbury Ave.
Kew Gardens
Surrey TW9 4JF England
Phone: 44 (0) 20 8392-8585;
Fax: 44 (0) 20 8392-9876
E-mail: info@bushwoodbooks.co.uk
Free postage in the U.K., Europe; air mail at cost.

Contents

Patios and Sitting Places for Wonderful Hours Outdoors

Cheery accents with colors and plants make living outdoors a pleasure for young and old. When one forms his fresh-air domicile as lovingly as his own home, letting the garden merge with the patio, the result is a harmonious transition with very unique charm.

Courage in creativity can also be shown by the surfaces of terraces and patios, for along with the surrounding plants, they essentially characterize the style and atmosphere of these green refuges.

It pays to choose patio and garden furniture according to comfort, style, size, material, color, and weather-resistance. A wealth of choice is ready to offer the right thing for any taste, whether chairs for pleasant socializing or lounging furniture for private, quiet happiness.

Even the smallest sitting places gain through the fluidity of lovely details. Fine containers, splendid plants, artistic vines, and magic garden happiness make it a small paradise.

Even the smallest city gardens and shady courtyards can be merged smoothly with the terrace or enchanting green sitting places. Shadowy plants in containers defy any surface, no matter how firmly paved, while fantastic pavement gives the surface an aesthetic charm even in winter.

With multi-faceted reflections and magic glitter, water lures the eye from terrace and sitting place, awakening the senses.

Surrounded by fragrant climbing vines, one can drift off to dreamland in enchanted groves, and enjoy mild nights and hot summer days in idylls just for two.

Whether hidden away among plants or dominating as an artistic attraction, pavilions crown the garden and can characterize certain areas with their own style. They offer the garden lover an enchanting atmosphere full of choice accessories, guaranteeing pleasure in any weather.

Patios

Living Comfort in Fresh-Air Oases

Unwinding begins directly outside the door when one can enjoy the magic of summer and its long evenings under dancing shadows of a sun-warmed ceiling of leaves. Undoubtedly, patios are places where life becomes a pleasure.

Variety for All Tastes

Patios allow us to experience the changing seasons first-hand, in the fresh air of the outdoors, yet close to the home. Naturally, one would not like to do without the comfort of a dwelling, nor the aesthetics of beautiful objects. Patios are open-air worlds borne by the wish for undisturbed privacy, and places where spare time can be spent unwinding or socializing. In a creative sense, though, patios represent the visual transitions between the house and the garden. With all their individual variety, they should nevertheless harmonize with both in terms of size, style, and materials.

A Place in the Sun

An important criterion for the formation, atmosphere, and use of a patio is its geographical layout.

—Patios in a southern position should not omit sunbathing surfaces. They absolutely need protection from the sun, too. As for building materials and furnishings, it is a good idea to avoid white and light colors, since they are blinding in glaring sunlight. Refreshing water fountains are recommended to deal with dry heat.

—Patios facing east get sunlight in the morning. This makes them ideal places to eat breakfast and to enjoy pleasant shade in the afternoon and evening during hot days. It is a good idea to install protection from a cold east wind.

—Patios facing west enchant as enjoyable after-work places, because they are bathed in golden light from afternoon to evening, and radiate absorbed heat into the night.

—Patios facing north are shady and offer pleasant coolness on hot days. Their disadvantage is that they warm up badly and stay damp long after rain. Thus one should avoid wooden surfaces, as they can become slippery. Friendly, bright colors are preferable for their decor.

Site and Size

The size of a patio is often determined by the layout of the lot and house. While rest areas could be laid out alongside freestanding houses, a single patio usually extends across the whole lot behind row houses.

The entrance to the garden is marked by an artistic gate in the midst of an evergreen hedge.

Slopes often make laying out flat surfaces difficult. Only through filling, terracing, or excavating the land can one gain more terrain for the patio. A square, circle, or not overly-narrow rectangle is recommended for use, because seating can best be arranged on them.

The entrance to a deeper-lying patio makes a stairway possible here, which adds color between the materials of the house and patio.

Here the back of the house allows a stage-like raised patio, located in a warmth-radiating area of the house and opening towards the garden on two sides.

Laid out in front of the building, this large patio swings out frontward to the garden in a striking semicircle. The patio features a stylish frame and is protected from wind by decorative sidewalls.

Influence of House and Garden

With every design, one faces the task of conceptualizing the patio as a living area that fulfills the wish for relaxation and enjoyment of life, and thus of using the spatial conditions advantageously.

Structural Elements Beside the House

The impression of safe solitude is brought about when a stay on the patio is not experienced as unprotected exposure. Thus on a patio that is linked with a house, one has a feeling of protection from behind, while lateral sight and wind shielding also promises security. Above all, though, a patio offers comfort with the addition of a roof to offer protection. An umbrella or a pergola can provide the same effect. Even partial covers, such as roof or balcony overhangs, loggias shielded as alcoves by house walls, or overhanging extensions can satisfy this need.

The Garden as a Frame

A patio that is completely or partially imbedded in the world of plants – by climbing vines, timbers, or framing beds with rosebushes or flowerbeds, contributes to one's sense of well-being.

A thorough joy for life through the soul and senses is only gained from a patio when it offers aesthetic enjoyment in addition to security. The view of the garden should be well composed, and the patio should flow harmoniously into the garden without hard lines or sharp angles.

This partly roofed patio attaches itself to the house and thus offers a place to spend spare time in a number of different activities.

Shielded by the house, this patio seems completely imbedded in the garden. The steps leading to the high ground level are thickly wreathed in wisteria (*Wisteria sinensis*), while the tasteful beds indulge the viewer with splendid shapes and colors.

Wide-crowned broadleaf trees close to the house can shield the patio like a canopy, giving it visual and spatial security. The green leafy roof filters the sunlight artistically and actively. Steps and platform offer additional places to sit and frame the lower seating area in the garden.

Raised Patio

Advantage: Better view of garden and surroundings.
Disadvantage: Without frame, sight, or wind shielding, one sits as if on a platter.
Tip: Form shields but keep view open.

Lowered Patio

Advantage: Homey seating imbedded in a protected small area.
Disadvantage: Often open view from above.
Tip: Limit the view with marquee, parasol, pergola, etc.

Raised Garden

Advantage: Low plants can wreath the top of the wall, fragrant plants are almost nose-high.
Disadvantage: Often no good view into the garden.
Tip: Put high plants in the background.

Variations in Lot Levels

A patio can occupy the same level as the house, but some lots require that it sit higher or lower. The same applies to the garden. A sloping lot can be a design headache when planning a patio and garden, demanding well thought-out solutions within reasonable cost limits.

One example: The house is often somewhat raised above the garden level. If one blends the patio level with the garden, the entrance to the patio from the house must be equipped with stairs. In this case, the patio can be extended any distance into the garden, surrounded by beds of fragrant flowers, or border a romantic pond or brook. The alternative consists of putting the patio on a stage above the garden. Then, as with all patios enclosed by shrubbery or set on a slope overlooking the garden, it is a matter of bedding it in and simultaneously sheltering it from wind and view. Vine-covered parapets and trellises, flowering shrubs or fragrant rosebushes, robust bushes or evergreen growths that can all be combined with each other provide an attractive means of doing so. Steep slopes with a rise or fall of fifty percent become "hanging gardens" when terraced with several small walls or palisades. Thus one gains beds for magical flower arrangements at various levels, which may also cover the crowns of vertical features. If the patio is above the garden, access must occur naturally via stairs. As beautiful as the view from a high position can be, one should be aware that the successful blending of bushes into a garden ensemble requires a lot of ability if one will not be satisfied with an ill-conceived rock garden, as is often seen on south-facing slopes.

Less is often more. That saying applies to this charming site with its pavement and wall that blend into the structure of the house.

Special Types of Patios

The patio does not always act as a connector between the house and garden. In places where space for the green of a garden is lacking, one need not do without a pleasant view into the outdoors. In cities, backyards are often transformed into patio areas, and roofs into roofed patios. But modern atrium houses, inspired by Oriental or Roman models, can also expand and develop a rich and scenic private world.

The Patio as a Garden Courtyard

This kind of patio is characterized by surrounding walls or, with atrium designs, house walls and windows. The smaller the surrounded area, the more one feels boxed in, and the higher the walls, the shadier the ground surface is. But if the space receives a lot of sunshine, its warming walls and pavement quickly develop dry air and shield one from heat. All this often makes problem children of inner courtyards, but with the addition of a few creative touches, refuges with flair can be developed.

Since the view cannot sweep into the garden as from other patios, and most often centers inwardly, the layout and furnishing of patio courtyards are of primary importance. The ground surface should blend with the house in material and design. Large surfaces should be divided spatially by raised beds and groups of plants into blocks, by

Between house and wall this shady place has developed, wreathed in green ivy and pipevine, its natural flair is enhanced by a raised pool with luxuriant water plants.

an alluring elfin glades or modern pools of water, trellis walls, or high wooden palisades. Trellises and mirror-like pools create the optical illusion of size or passage in small yards, eliminating that boxed-in feeling. Walls can be magically clothed with robust flower growths like Clematis and roses or evergreen ivy, which thrive especially well where the air is moist. Above all, splashing water from small wall fountains, waterfalls, or spring stones can have a magical effect and turn the patio into an idyllic and lively spot. And of course, furniture, grill, and containers should add to the prevailing style.

Tip

Forming Patio Courtyards

The elements at a glance:
—Pavements that match house and walls
—Water in the form of wall fountains and springs, bowls and courses, stone fountains
—Attractive wall elements that add flair even in winter
—Decorative flowerpots
—Climbing vines
—Plants that add shade and thrive in dry air

The stairs not only give access to the veranda, but also afford living space for a lively assortment of plants.

Small but elegant is this glass-roofed gallery with a view of colorful potted plants and climbing vines.

Open-Air Galleries and Verandas

Sets of steps against the house that lead to an entrance can be transformed into a veranda – a roofed sitting place beside the house, sheltered from wind and weather by walls of glass. On noble estates, large patio plateaus often feature nostalgic stone balustrades or coverings that resemble a winter garden. Besides shelter, these also offer the raised patio a charming frame and provide plenty of niches where you can place ornamental flowers.

The furnishing of such patios will also depend on how much they are or are not exposed to the weather. In protected, roofed areas, one can enjoy basket chairs of willow, bamboo, or rattan. Places exposed to rain, like roof patios, require a surface as skid-free as possible.

Amid structural elements, rich green can lure the soul and senses. Sunny patios can offer little gardens for snacks as well as flowery paradises, and nightly centers of pleasure with herbs and fragrant plants. Dark places, on the other hand, appear magically brightened by white or pastel flowers that thrive in shade, like Fuchsia or Busy Lizzie (*Impatiens* New Guinea or the rose-like *Impatiens walleriana* hybrids).

Robust climbing vines such as Anemone Clematis (*Clematis montana*), Climbing Hydrangea (*Hydrangea anomala* ssp. *petiolaris*), Russian Vine (*Fallopia baldschuanica*), and Honeysuckle (*Lonicera* species) also grow well in the shade, while English Ivy (*Hedera helix*) and Boston Ivy (*Parthenocissus tricuspidata* 'Veitchii'), being self-supporting climbers, need no help on vertical walls. Any of them can be planted at the foot of walls or stairs and will climb up.

You can add green to raised patios:
—With potted plants on the stairs
—With hanging plants dangling from the roof
—With strong climbing plants on the handrails or the wall
—With hanging plants in pots by the rail, balustrade or wall.

Roof Patios

These green oases above the roofs of the city often afford fascinating panoramas. But before one takes initiative and begins the work, an architect must be hired to examine the sturdiness and load limit of the roof, as well as find means of insulating it properly.

Roof patios are generally exposed to sun, wind, and rain, and thus they require weather-resistant furnishings and plant containers. Of primary importance is shelter from the wind, which can be checked by evergreen bushes and stable walls made of wood or stone. Because of stronger winds at greater heights, one should set all the plants in stable containers, making sure to weigh down the root areas of taller plants with large stones. Since wind and sun also dry out the soil in flowerpots very quickly, it is a good idea not to group plants together in larger boxes, rather than set them individually in pots or bowls. Mobile furnishings such as umbrellas, awnings, and marquees, or a covering pergola with climbing vines, must be well anchored in the case of high-wind conditions.

In the airy heights of a roof patio, plants that can stand hot sun and strong wind will thrive. These include Serviceberry (*Amelanchier lamarckii*), English Yew (*Taxus baccata*), Scarlet Firethorn (*Pyracantha coccinea)*, Bush Cinquefoil (*Potentilla fruticosa*), Wintercreeper Euonymus (*Euonymus fortunei*), Lavender (*Lavandula angustifolia*), and ground-covering roses.

This raised sitting place under a yellow parasol lies beside the house like a roof patio.

In blue-violet, white, and green, the potted plants enhance the blue of the house.

"Over all the treetops is still." Nowhere can the many shades of blue in an evening sky be enjoyed more fully than on a roof patio – provided one selects the right place for the seats with the best view.

A Patio Inventory

On patios, carefree moods and a relaxed, happy spirit of life can be manifested with the addition of the right furnishings and artistic touches. Before you set out to find the perfect patio accessories, you should determine exactly what you want, choosing items based on their potential for realization as a whole, and perhaps give up special desires in favor of practicality. It should also be considered that a furnished patio consists both of fundamental elements that should serve and satisfy over long periods of time, and of mobile accessories that can be moved here or there, some that may only enrich a single season with their charm.

A masterpiece of ground surface. Plants that gently reflect the edges and a decorative ornament make the patio a joy to behold.

Before doing any building, the job should be thoroughly thought out, planned, and stylistically harmonized. Great importance should be devoted to the transition from the patio to the garden. The lines and contours of the patio can highlight, embellish, or overcome the style of house and garden. Thus, patio borders that fit into formal gardens or form semicircles can add a firm line to the garden. The more romantic or natural the house and garden are, the more the green can flow into the patio. Row-house patios in particular appear livelier and larger when they blend into the garden irregularly with swinging contours or separate surfaces. Even abrupt breaks like low enclosing walls can be softened with climbing vines or plants growing from boxes.

Practical structures too, like grills or storage cabinets for cushions or gardening utensils, must be planned more carefully when less space is available. The first priority, though, goes to the sitting and lying furniture. One should plan on at least 30-45 square feet for a sitting area, and 90-150 square feet for chaise-lounges and a grill. On particularly extensive patios, even a swimming pool with a changing cabin can be included.

If the structural elements complement one another, the mobile elements add the last homey touch to the paradise at your backdoor. Furniture and textiles, plants and ornate flowerpots, ornaments and light create atmosphere and lifestyle on the patio. They should harmonize with their surroundings in color, shape, and style, whether they blend closely, strike lively accents, or contrast deliberately to develop a vital, unique life.

This patio wreathed in blue expresses coziness and harmony. The house and garden provide a frame matched by the tablecloth and cushions.

Rectangular plates are laid close together.

Irregular plates have wide interstices.

Classic Surfaces

Many garden owners too infrequently utilize the charming reflections and patterns of natural and artificial stone. It is surprising the myriad ways different materials form surfaces by their:
—Size and shape (stone, pavement)
—Finishes
—Colors (depending on material)
—Layout design
—And interstice width.

The patio surface should fit in with the house and garden, and if possible, also be repeated in other garden elements like paths or seats. It should be strong and weight-supporting, resistant to weather and frost, as well as safe to walk on without slipping. A wide variety of plates and paving stones of frost-resistant natural materials are available, plus concrete pavers, cinder blocks and bricks, and wooden planks or panels. It is important that every patio surface be sloped two degrees to lead water away from the house.

Cut Shaped Plates

Stones and plates of uniform size are usually laid in a cross-lined pattern. It looks stable and strong. Polished plates go well with modern and elegant city architecture.

Broken & Sawn Plates

The wild union of such plates looks lively and organic. It looks good in free-form or natural gardens. Strict enclosures with rolling layers give it a sense of calm.

Wooden planks form a restful deck surface.

Various shades of granite liven up this pavement.

Bricks or cinder blocks line up regularly.

Plate Surfaces

Very harmonious transitions to the garden succeed with frost-resistant, natural stone plates, which are available in geometrical shapes or irregular (polygonal) forms. They are considerably more costly than concrete blocks, which are likewise available in various sizes, shapes, and surface types. Before buying them, one should layout a few blocks at the site and dampen them to test their color and resistance to slipping when wet.

Small Paving Stones

Natural stone, concrete, cinder block, frost-free brick, or gravel in various sizes can form charming patterns – particularly circles, arches, or small corners. They can make a surface not only very lively, but also create perspective effects according to how they are arranged. Another advantage: The terrain is fixed but not completely sealed, and the rainwater can drain well between the cracks.

Wooden Planks

They harmonize well with the garden's green and should be chosen for sunny terraces, since they become slippery when wet. Boards laid crossways with lengthwise cracks are somewhat safer.

Natural Stone Pavement

Running rows include equally large stones and plates with regular interstices. Rectangular stones look longer or wider when running lengthwise or crosswise.

Cinder-Block Pavement

Cinder blocks can be purchased in many flat or curved patterns, and should always be stabilized with an edge of arched or vertically laid pieces.

Bricks or cinder blocks that also cover the low wall, granite paving stones in varying sizes, and colorful ceramic tiles give this little sitting place a strikingly original design. To give such striking pavements their deserved advantage, the furniture should go well with them.

Charming Mixes of Materials

While many garden lovers spare no effort to fill the garden with a blossoming sea of shapes and colors, the loving adornment of solid surfaces – such as paths, sitting places, and particularly patios – is only gradually gaining a similarly high priority. This is astonishing, for while planting is usually limited by time to a seasonal high point, the surface of a patio is in view at any season. Whoever approaches the realm of pavement will be amazed at the sparkling effect of this art form. Regular combinations, patterns, and an inexhaustible variety of possible blends form a treasure chest for individual creation. One can combine:

—The same material in different shapes and sizes (for example, large and small granite paving stones).
—The same material in varying colors, as can be done with granite, gneiss, and sandstone.
—Different materials in various forms but the same color. Thus concrete slabs take on a new charm when surrounded by small granite paving stones, gravel, or crushed stone walks.
—Different materials in various shapes and colors, such as reddish polygonal porphyry plates with silvery granite paving stones.
—Customary materials with brightly colored frost-resistant, baked mosaic stones or ceramic tiles, best suited for ornamental or focal-point scattering.
—Customary materials and frost-resistant flagstones, old iron pieces, crushed stone, ceramic and glass pieces, and other recycled materials formed into a mosaic.

Patios near a house should also be cleared in winter to change the view without spreading uneasiness. It looks especially harmonious when the materials, patterns, or ornaments used on it also recur in the garden.

Whoever prefers wooden surfaces must not feel limited to lengthwise or transverse planks. They can also be laid diagonally to the area, form one or more central ribs, or be used as panels, groups of blocks, or diagonals.

The classic frieze motif in dark colors is integrated into the patio surface. Large paving stones in the same format but varying colors can achieve this restful mood in normal blends.

Framed by roof tiles on edge and bricks, old building material was artistically formed into fanciful mosaics.

Tried and True Sources of Shade

While one greets the first sunbeams of spring with a hunger for light, their power from May on can make life harder on south-facing patios. Shade is needed to avoid glaring light, UV rays, and oppressive heat. How nice that one can choose between mobile and fixed sources of shade.

Flexible shade is provided by umbrellas, round or square, in various sizes and colors that can add midsummer magic. Alas, they require a surface to stand on or block direct eye contact in the midst of chairs and tables. On the other hand, fixed marquees on houses require no foot room, but are extended by knob or crank and generally span the full width of the patio. Colorful fabrics bathe the patio in tinted light. Whoever chooses them should match their colors with the house, garden, and patio. Tent canvas or awnings, likewise attached to the house and extending forward, are usually creamy-white and stay up for the whole summer. Marquees and awnings are also very popular in heavily populated areas because they block the view from above.

A widely-crowned broadleaf tree before the patio, or a pergola alive with climbing vines can also provide enduring and airy shade from the sun. Roofed pergolas "plant their feet" at the edge of the patio or on the pavement. When climbing vines, such as rambling roses (*Rosa*), Clematis (*Clematis*), Honeysuckle (*Lonicera*) or Wisteria (*Wisteria*), are planted there in a bed or in cutouts of the pavement, one can soon enjoy their aroma even from some distance away. One can use pressure-treated round or angled wood, which can also be glazed, as well as nostalgic or modern steel components. But pergolas of two materials also look enchanting, for example, natural stone, cinder-block or concrete supports with wooden or metal extensions.

Under the inviting shadow of a sunshade, the greatest heat cannot disturb pleasant summer days in the garden.

A pergola attached to the house, with its supports linked by posts on which the rafters rest.

Patios lying in front of the house, like roof patios, are fully exposed to the sun. A large tent fabric of cool white offers beneficial shade without hindering air circulation.

Much like an extendable marquee, a wide fabric awning hung beneath a glass roof creates light shadow here.

Trees before the patio function as eye-catchers that give depth to a garden with spatially ordered plantings. They cast emotionally moving plays of light and shadow below the green roof of leaves.

When a natural country-house style typifies the patio and its denizens, then a rustic woodpile crowned by a gallery of flowers gives privacy to the comfortable seating area and deflects curious stares.

The semitransparent privacy screen of white laths is a restful counterpoint to the lively pavement.

The luxuriant Wisteria not only covers the stairs in green but also keeps out unwanted drafts.

Charming Shields from Wind and Sight

In order for patios to be considered refuges for withdrawal from everyday life, they must offer peaceful relaxation to solitude-seekers, as well as provide privacy to social gatherings. One cannot deny the appeal of shutting off disturbances from outside by shielding oneself from strange eyes and chilly breezes.

Walls With Special Effects

Walls, as extensions of house walls with their length fitting the patio, are popular because they also shut out noise. If they are extended onward through the garden to the end of the property, an assortment of plants in front of them or climbing vines on them is recommended. But where they flank the patio, it is a matter of integrating them sensibly and decoratively into the outside living area. Charming possibilities exist:

—When walls are covered with trellises for vines, they have a capricious charm even in winter. From decorative pots below these trellises, annual vines can exhibit their flowery splendor anew every summer. It has a particularly idyllic effect when their containers are chosen from the start to harmonize in form, color, and style. Depending on the style of patio and house, they can be nostalgic types, classic stone containers, or modern designs with severe steel containers or minimal concrete troughs.

Trellises have an ever-nicer effect with a gently flowing end that leads to an accent, for example, a pillar with a ball, pine cone, or planter bowl.

Plant Name	Location	Blossoms	Height	Water	Care
Trailing Snapdragon *Asarina barclaiana*	sun to partial shade	June to October	6-9ft. (2-3m)	abundant	fertilize weekly
Balloon Vine *Cardiospermum halicacaburn*	sunny, moist	Fruit from June	6-9ft. (2-3m)	abundant	fertilize biweekly
Cup and Saucer Vine *Cobaea scandens*	sunny, moist	August to October	5-6ft. (1.8-2m)	abundant	fertilize weekly
Pumpkin *Cucurbita pepo*	sunny, warm, moist soil	July to August	6-9ft. (2-3m)	abundant	fertilize
Chilean Glory Flower *Eccremocarpus scaber*	sunny	July to October	6-12ft. (2-4m)	moderate, keep moist	fertilize every 4 weeks
Japanese Hops *Humulus japonicus*	sunny	July to August	12-18ft. (4-6m)	moderate, keep moist	none
Morning Glory *Ipomoea lobata*	sunny, sheltered	July to September	12-15ft. (4-5m)	moderate, keep moist	fertilize weekly
Morning Glory *Ipomoea tricolor*	sunny, sheltered	July to September	7-9ft. (2.5-3m)	moderate, keep moist	fertilize every 3 weeks
Morning Glory *Ipomoea purpurea*	sunny	July to September	6-9ft. (2-3m)	moderate, keep moist	fertilize every 3 weeks
Lablab Bean *Lablab purpureus*	sunny, sheltered	September to October	9-12ft. (3-4m)	well, keep moist	fertilize every 2-3 weeks
Bottle Gourd *Lagenaria siceraria*	sunny, moist	June to September	7-9ft. (2.5-3m)	abundant	fertilize weekly
Sweet Pea *Lathyrus odoratus*	sun to partial shade	June to September	1-6ft. (0.5-2m)	keep fairly moist	fertilize every 3 weeks
Scarlet Runner Bean *Phaseolus coccineus*	sunny, sheltered	July to September	6-12ft. (3-4m)	keep fairly moist	fertilize every 3 weeks
Purple Bells *Rhodochiton atrosanguineus*	sunny	August to October	7-9ft. (2.5-3m)	keep fairly moist	fertilize weekly
Black-Eyed Susan *Thunbergia alata*	sunny, warm	May to October	3-5ft. (1-1.5m)	abundant	fertilize every 2 weeks
Garden Nasturtium *Tropaeolum majus*	sunny, warm, sheltered	July to October	6-9ft. (2-3m)	keep fairly moist	fertilize every 4 weeks
Canary Creeper *Tropaeolum peregrinum*	sunny, warm, sheltered	July to October	9-12ft. (3-4m)	keep moist	fertilize every 4 weeks

—Charming views or niches exist in walls that are pierced by decorative windows or medallions. They let in light from the side and paint artistic stripes of light on the patio surface.
—The joyful splashing of wall fountains enlivens the patio with acoustic attraction. They can also be installed on solid walls with burlesque reservoirs, catch basins, pumps, and pipes.
—On small patios, *trompe-l'oeil* performs optical tricks to suggest distance. Examples of this are mirrors, windows, or doors surrounded by vines, using perspective illusions on the flat surface to hint at idyllic spaces behind them.

Evergreen ivy and wild grapes are a pleasant team of climbers that can offer fantastic autumn color in green and red.

To guarantee privacy from the front use:
—**Evergreen trees, such as Box-tree, Holly** (*Ilex*), Yew (*Taxus*)
—**Beds with artistically trained trees**
—**Bushy roses**
—**Obelisks or pyramids with climbing plants like Clematis and roses**
—**Pergolas with a single vine-covered spar, allowing views into the garden.**

Trellis Walls for Green Acrobats

Wooden constructions can also serve as lateral windbreaks and sight screens. Some of them, such as palisades, woven walls, or reed mats, completely cut off any view, while others are semitransparent like trellises, which become more shielding only when richly overgrown with vines. Wooden trellises with their many varieties of patterns, shapes, and heights, can be painted brightly to match window or door frames, textiles, containers, plants, or furniture on the patio. Thus, even in winter, after the leaves fall, they brighten the scene with refreshing color. They also gain ornamental charm when they are integrated into stately pergolas.

Nostalgic, ivy-covered walls of layered steel pipe form airier screens that recall the bewitching magic of old English gardens. In general, one should be lavish with vines and climbers, for they are part of the screen all year round.

Green Walls as Living Architecture

Trimmed hedges can also flank patios, serve as screens and deflect the wind. However, they require more space than climbing vines, and must be trimmed exactly from each side at least once a year. If one chooses evergreen shrubs like Yew or Arbor Vitae, fresh green brightens up the screen even in winter.

Seating Comfort for All Tastes

The patio is an outdoor dwelling, a place for relaxation and sociability that allows one to enjoy the flair of days and seasons in full measure. The contribution of the furniture is not to be undervalued, for its comfort and aesthetics make sweet idleness complete. Patio and garden chairs and armchairs, benches, and tables should be chosen sensibly by formative criteria, as should be furnishings for pure relaxation, such as couches, recliners, chaise-lounges, and rocking chairs.

Patio furniture is exposed to different forces than interior furniture. Sunlight, humidity, and great temperature changes stress materials and workmanship even on roofed patios. If the furniture is exposed to rain and snow, only special materials are suitable.

Patio Furniture should be:
—Comfortable, which means offering comfort while sitting, eating, or reclining
—Aesthetically complementary with the house and patio in style, size, material, and color
—Practical and purposeful, which means easy to care for and resistant to weather.

More Than a Question of Taste

Garden furniture is the central element of the patio and thus should be chosen calmly, with intuitive feeling, and above all, only after a sitting test. When the patio harmonizes with the style of the house, they become visually linked. Wooden or wicker furniture suits a rural domicile wonderfully, but not modern aluminum design. Neither is it recommended to adorn the patio of a building of simple elegance with an overstated, 19th-century style cast-iron ensemble.

A restrained design of aluminum and wickerwork typifies the subtle furnishings by the house, where gentle natural tones are also found in the massive deck chairs of teak.

The elegant woven chairs are light and thus easy to move. Colorfully painted, they can also withstand a brief rain shower.

An ode to design is this futuristic armchair, which its designer, Jasper Morrison, called the "Thinking Man's Chair."

All-around artist Philippe Starck made his enchanting "Lord Yo" chairs of plastics.

Modern, functional, and stackable is this lightweight aluminum ensemble.

A Little Knowledge of Materials

The workmanship and style of furniture are often closely linked with the materials.

—Wooden furniture is available in many price ranges. Whoever would like to enjoy it for a long time should definitely choose a hardwood, such as locust, red cedar, or plantation teak. These fine-grained hardwoods need no care, last very long in sun, rain, frost, and snow, and take on a nice silver-gray patina after a short time. The classic teak pieces designed after English models with their fine character fit into city and country patios alike, as long as they are not too small.

—Metal furniture of heavy cast iron is generally a decorative throwback to the 19th century. Others express Mediterranean charm or the flair of French bistro culture. This type of furniture is readily available, can be treated to resist rust, and comes in various colors. Steel tube, iron, and weather-resistant aluminum in strong functional designs complement a variety of styles very well.

—Woven furniture of rush, rattan, and bamboo offer nostalgic comfort or Far Eastern flair. They should be kept in a sheltered place, as should the light loom-chairs made of paper twisted and glued with wire that provide transparent elegance to any space. New on the market are exquisite woven furnishings made from synthetic materials like the permanent Hularo plastic fibers that even snow cannot harm.

—As for plastic furniture, one should select high quality that can withstand any storm.

—Very popular at this time are combinations of materials such as teak with iron, stainless steel, aluminum, or aluminum along with plastic in popular designs.

With cushions and tablecloths that reflect or contrast with the tones of their surroundings, additional color changes and accents can be created on the patio.

This comfortable folding furniture of iron and teak expresses a spare-time mood in its loveliest form.

Perfectly harmonious in weathered silver gray is this teak furniture on a wooden deck.

This patio is surrounded by flowering shrubs like roses and Weigelia, plus bushes in pastel shades, forming a gentle natural wreath.

Plant Arabesques as Frames

The floral splendor planted in beds or in the lawn around the patio has the important job of linking the patio with the garden. When the specialist speaks of this link, he means two things:

—The plantings should be laid out so that they serve as sensual high points to attract the eye from the patio into the depths of the garden. In this way the garden is drawn into the patio user's awareness and subtly linked to the patio.

—At the same time, the plantings in front of the patio, seen from the garden, should lead the green area toward the house.

Creating a spirited atmosphere with plantings around the patio should be the highest priority for any garden fan, as the relaxing value of this outdoor seating is also measured in the amount of aesthetic joy offered by the surroundings. The possibilities are simply endless, but in individual cases they depend on the placement, light and shadow, style and size of the garden, as well as the owner's tastes.

On sunny patios the fragrant sea of flowers in a long-blooming bed is of primary importance. Unfortunately, this requires much gardening skill and years of experience. Beginners can get by with a simple trick: One creates always-green islands in the bed which look good even when not blooming, and surrounds them with summer flowers, bushes, or roses. Suitable green plants include the European Box-tree (*Buxus sempervirens*) or the similar Japanese Holly (*Ilex crenata*), which lend color and structure to the garden even in winter. Other possibilities are evergreen shrubs such as Chinese Peony (*Paeonia lactiflora* hybrids), Bearded Iris (*Iris barbata* hybrids), Live-forever (*Sedum tlephium*), or Lavender (*Lavandula angustifolia*). Depending on the width of the bed, one should add steppingstones that make care easier.

Plants of varying height levels are important elements in all horizontal beds, as they lead the eye upward and add dimension to the garden. Decorative shrubs can provide beauty at various times of the year, with their blossoms and autumn colors. Some examples include Witch Hazel (*Hamamelis* hybrids), Corkscrew Hazel (*Corylus avellana* "Contorta"), decorative crabapples (*Malus* varieties), and ornamental cherries (*Prunus* varieties). Taller, solitary trees with shade-giving crowns are also suitable in larger gardens.

Lavender and roses not only form an alluring combination visually, but also enchant patios with the fragrance of their blossoms. Before they bloom in early summer, earlier-blooming bulb flowers can open the season.

Artistic freestanding climbing elements hung with roses, Clematis, Honeysuckle, or annual climbers can be fascinating points of sight-screening or colorful eyecatchers before patios.

Never put plants in rows. Grouped by variations in height – even with the help of pots and planters – they have the most charming effect.

Patios in high positions often need wind and sight shielding, which can be achieved by planting a variety of taller shrubs, or by constructing a pergola with openings that allow you to see beyond it.

In formal gardens, box-trees can frame the beds, their cubes or spheres creating a striking effect. Shrubs, roses, and bushes can provide ambiance when they swing into the patio and mask the angles of the pavement.

Mobile Gardens Full of Fragrance and Color

Who can resist the magic of plants? If the garden is small, green plants can gather around the patio to create a colorful rendezvous. In pails and boxes, pots and bowls, glass containers and amphorae one can raise an astounding variety of floral treasures. The anxiety of choice is reduced for every patio owner, for he must first make two decisions.

First, does the patio offer growing plants predominantly sun or shade? Accordingly, such plants whose needs are met by this patio should be chosen.

Second, does one want a rich and changing, season-long planting or a lasting ensemble of plants that will be a constant companion on the patio throughout the year? In this case one must decide whether suitable winter quarters are ready for the potted plants – frost-sensitive beauties from Mediterranean or tropical climes. If this is not the case, one should choose shrubs, bushes, grasses and ferns that winter well as all-year guests that thrive in pots and can overwinter on the patio with some protection.

Robust Long-Term Plantings

Among the countless shrubs, dwarf conifers are very competitive in the autumn, but also show presence and color on the patio in the winter. Many of them blossom early in the spring, so one can choose flowering shrubs that offer changing attractions through the seasons.

Flowering Shrubs as Potted Plants

- **Hortensia** (*Hydrangea* hybrids)
- **Flowering Quince** (*Chaenomeles* hybrids)
- **Serviceberry** (*Amelanchier* varieties)
- **Pussy Willow** (*Salix caprea 'Pendula'*)
- **Bush Cinquefoil** (*Potentilla fruticosa*)
- **Dwarf Bed Roses** (*Rosa* varieties)
- **Autumn Lilacs** (*Syringa microphylla*)

Hortensia (*Hydrangea* hybrids), with its decorative, long-blooming, round flowers, and Japanese Maple (*Acer palmatum*), with its graceful form and fiery autumn color, can thrive in pots on the patio for many years.

A small *objet d'art* is this shadowed patio wreathed in green. Between rounded boxwood and spherical yew with evergreen Pachysandra at their feet, one reaches a seat crowned with Funkia (*Hosta* hybrids) and Hortensia (*Hydrangea* hybrids).

With a tender green they welcome the new year, and later they complete the yearly cycle with borders of blooming splendor, decorative fruition, and autumn colors. Evergreen broadleaf shrubs such as Boxwood (*Buxus sempervirens*), English Holly (*Ilex aquifolium*), Japanese Holly (*Ilex crenata*), and English Yew (*Taxus baccata*) can adorn any patio, for they adapt well to its formative elements (topiary).

Bushes also give a patio transitory color, depending on their blossoming time. A classic choice for use in containers are the Funkias, with their ornamental leaves, existing not only in juicy green but also blue-green, yellow-green, or with fine, yellow stripes. They can overwinter in pots but should be covered with brushwood and watered on frost-free days so their roots will not dry out. It is even better to plant the bushes in a cleared-out bed in the autumn.

A good tip, not only for beds, involves the fairy-like ornamental grasses. Many can be raised very well in pots in sunny places. Some include Japanese Mountain Grass (*Hakonechloa macra*), Blue Oat-grass (*Helictotrichon sempervirens*), Purple Moor-grass (*Molinia caerulea*), and Chinese Fountain Grass (*Pennisetum alopecuroides*). In shady areas one can plant yellow-bordered evergreen Japanese Sedge (*Carex morrowii 'Variegata'*).

One should not forget that in order to survive cold winters, the containers as well as the plants should be absolutely impervious to winter.

Sun-loving Bushes for Potting

- **Catnip** (*Nepeta x faassenii*)
- **Live-forever** (*Sedum telephium*)
- **Yarrow** (*Achillea* hybrids)
- **Adam's Needle-and-Thread** (*Yucca filamentosa*)
- **Bearded Iris** (*Iris barbata* hybrids)
- **Day Lily** (*Hemerocallis* hybrids)
- **Horned Violet** (*Viola cornuta*)
- **Sun Rose** (*Helianthemum*)

While a Wisteria winds its way around a small tree in a cutout of the pavement, a Mediterranean society of Rosemary, Sage, Zist Rose, and Geranium makes itself at home, enriching the patio with a mobile island of fragrance.

Flower growers also use a patio for their collections of special plants, such as these sun-hungry Houseleek (*Sempervivium*) varieties.

Plant Name	Location	Blossoms	Color	Water	Care
Bacopa, Snow Flake *Sutera cordata**	sunny	May to October	white, blue	fairly moist	fertilize every 2 weeks
Begonia *Begonia x tuberhydr.***	part shade	May to October	white, yellow to red	fairly moist	fertilize every 2 weeks
Tickseed *Bidens ferulifolia**	sunny	June to September	yellow	abundant	fertilize every 2 weeks
River Daisy *Brachyscome iberidifolia**	sunny	May to September	white, red, violet	abundant	fertilize every 3 weeks
Ground Morning Glory *Convolvulus sabatius**	sunny	June to October	blue-violet	moderate	fertilize every 4 weeks
Twin Spur *Diascia barberae*	sunny	May to October	light to dark rose	keep evenly moist	fertilize every 4 weeks
Blue Marguerite *Felicia amelloides*	sunny	May to October	blue with yellow center	moderate	fertilize every 4 weeks
Fuchsia *Fuchsia hybrids**	part shade, shade	May to October	white, rose, red, violet	abundant	fertilize every 3 weeks
Licorice Plant *Helichrysum petiolare**	sunny to part shade	decorative leaves	silvery, velvety	moderate	fertilize every 4 weeks
Busy Lizzie *Impatiens newguinea and walleriana hybrids*	part shade	May to October	white, red, violet, salmon	keep evenly moist	fertilize every 2 weeks
Edging Lobelia *Lobelia erinus**	sunny to part shade	May to October	white, rose, blue, lilac	keep evenly moist	fertilize every 3 weeks
Sweet Alyssum *Lobularia maritima**	sun to shade	May to October	white, rose, red-violet	moderate	fertilize every 4 weeks
Geranium *Pelargonium hybrids***	sun to part shade	May to October	white, rose, red	keep evenly moist	fertilize every 2 weeks
Petunia *Petunia surfinia hybrids, Miniature Petunia "Million Bells" ***	sunny	May to October	white, rose, yellow, red	abundant	fertilize every 3 weeks
Fan Flower *Scaevola saligna**	sunny to part shade	May to October	blue-violet	evenly limed	fertilize every 3 weeks
Vervain *Verbena hybrids*	sunny	June to October	white, rose, red, lilac	abundant	fertilize every 2 weeks

*Hanging
**Hanging or potted

Flowers for Every Season

Annual summer and balcony flowers usually produce a sea of blossoms from May into the autumn. It is no wonder that they are so popular on patios, spreading color and tender fragrance galore. Another advantage is that planting can be done in no time, using young plants grown by a gardener – and since their pots are free in the spring, as well as in the autumn and winter, they can be filled year-round with seasonal flowers. Hothouse spring flowers such as Primulas, Crocus, Dwarf Narcissus, Hyacinths, and Tulips, once transplanted, naturally need to be protected with burled foil on frosty days and nights.

Mobile Color and Theme Gardens

Quick seasonal plantings not only provide blossoms through spring, summer, and autumn, but also allow one to play with color. Harmonious scenes are formed particularly when hues from house or garden are repeated, avoiding an excess of colors. Arrangements that are limited to one or two colors, warm or cool tones, or tender pastel shades are particularly striking.

Vegetables and many herbs are also grown annually. Almost all are suitable for potting, so that they can create the most alluring theme gardens in combination with other types of plants.

How about an herb garden right next to the kitchen door? Or a mobile snack garden with strawberries, radishes, peas, tomatoes and many other fresh picks that lift young hearts? Young single or double households can supply their kitchen with fresh produce from a gourmet garden of greens, such as Japanese mizuna or Italian rucola, Thai basil, and fresh climbing zucchini. A fragrant patio with roses and lilacs, lavender and lilies, carnations, stock, heliotrope, and the sweet perfume of Angel's Trumpet in pots provides much pleasure. Along with the fine lemon aroma of citrus plants and lemon-scented verbena, they make a visit to the patio an alluring feast of the senses. A very different character is provided by a farm garden with nasturtiums and marigolds, sunflowers, tomatoes, and lettuce.

Southern fragrances are spread here by Lavender, Rosemary, Oregano, and Geranium, which give their charm to a niche with an idyllic potted garden.

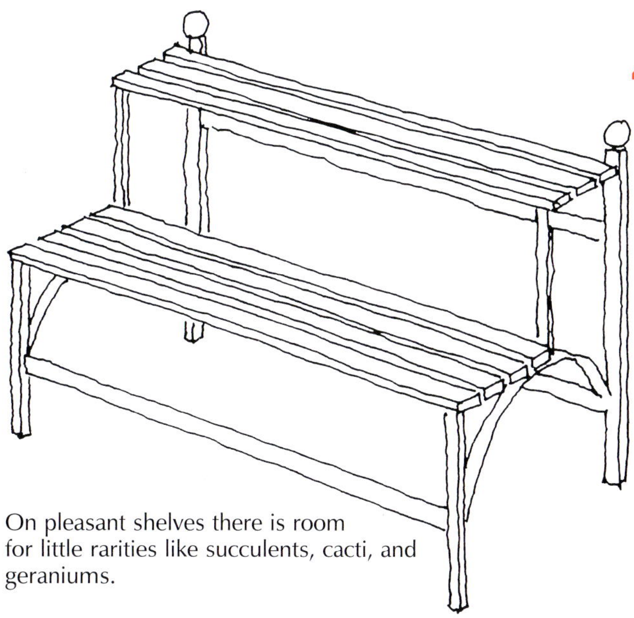

On pleasant shelves there is room for little rarities like succulents, cacti, and geraniums.

Plant Name	Location	Blossoms	Water	Fertilize	Overwinter
Bellflower *Abutilon* hybrids	bright, not full sun	April to October	abundant	weekly to August	light 40-50° F (5-10°C)
Lily of the Valley *Agapanthus praecox*	sunny to part shade	July to August	abundant	weekly to August	light 32-50°F (0-10°C)
Lemon Verbena *Aloysia triphylla*	sunny to part shade	July to September	abundant	biweekly to August	light or dark 40-50°F (5-10°C)
Marguerite *Argyranthemum frutescens*	sunny	May to October	abundant	weekly to August	light 40-50°F (5-10°C)
Bougainvillea *Bougainvillea hybrids*	sunny	May to August	abundant	weekly to August	light 40-50°F (5-10°C)
Datura/Angel's Trumpet *Brugmansia aurea*	sunny to part shade	June to September	abundant	weekly to August	light or dark 40-50°F (5-10°C)
Red Cestrum *Cestrum elegans*	sunny	May to September	abundant	weekly to August	dark 40-50°F (5-10°C)
Lemon, Orange *Citrus limon, Citrus sinensis*	sunny	all year	moderate	weekly to August	light 40-50°F (5-10°C)
Coral Tree *Erythrina crista-galli*	sunny	July to September	moderate	monthly to August	dark 40-50°F (5-10°C)
Hibiscus *Hibiscus rosa-sinensis*	sunny to part shade	March to October	abundant	weekly to August	light, room temperature
Common Lantana *Lantana camara hybrids*	sunny	May to October	abundant	biweekly to August	light 40-50°F (5-10°C)
Gentian Bush *Lycianthes rantonetti*	sunny to part shade	July to October	abundant	weekly to August	dark 40-50°F (5-10°C)
Oleander *Nerium oleander*	sunny	June to October	abundant	weekly to October	light 40-50°F (5-10°C)
Olive Tree *Olea europaea*	sunny	July to August	minimal, well-drained soil	biweekly to August	light or dark 32-50°F (0-10 °C)
Blue Plumbago *Plumbago auriculata*	sunny	June to October	abundant	weekly to August	light or dark 40-50°F (5-10 °C)
Pomegranate *Punica granatum*	sunny	June to August	abundant	monthly to August	light or dark 40-50°F (5-10 °C)
Chaste Tree *Vitex agnus-castus*	sunny	August to October	abundant	biweekly to August	light or dark 15-60°F (5-15°C)

Potted plants such as Lily of the Nile (*Agapanthus praecox*) crown seats with their mysterious blue color, but can just as well highlight bare walls, staircases, and passages.

Exotic Dreams

Potted plants are guests from faraway lands. They grow to be much larger shrubs (very few of them are bushes) in their native lands than in a necessary pot in our climate. Too little light and warmth, and too-cold, dark winters cause many plants to endure a bare existence unless the knowledgeable gardener helps them along. If a place where they can overwinter is available, then the work is worth doing. This work includes placing them in an ever-larger and heavier pot in the autumn, removing and repotting the charming giants in the spring, and caring for them devotedly all year round. According to their origin, they bring the flair of Mediterranean life, exotic mysteries, and the restraining extravagance of succulent plants to the patio, and thus contribute in passing to the vacation mood at home.

Since potted plants are not plants to be discarded, whoever selects them should have chosen in advance to care for them over a long period as well. The plants thank us with their annually growing beauty. Additionally, we should consider that:

—Small, delicate young plants can grow large by the season's end, and in time they will require much room on the patio and in their winter quarters.

—Less is often more. One should not place potted plants too close together in summer or winter. Rather, buy fewer plants and integrate them with balcony plants.

—Many potted plants (such as Marguerite, Datura, Hibiscus, Lantana, Oleander, Olive, Plumbago, Pomegranate, Gentian Bush, etc.) can be grown tall, taking up less space. They attract attention, especially if one surrounds their bare feet with balcony flowers.

An extensive patio by a pool with a walk around it.

A fountain at the entrance to the garden.

A wall fountain takes up very little space.

A small basin with a lively fountain.

Multi-Faceted Bodies of Water

Seats and water belong together. Whoever brings water into the garden also wants to enjoy it. For this reason one likes to build ponds near the patio in a small garden – though not only there – where one can sit on the deck and give oneself over to the magic of fluid elements, observe their reflection and glitter along with the special world of plants and animals. On hot days, other positive qualities of ponds become tangible: They increase the air humidity, give out a refreshing coolness during the day, and pleasantly exude stored-up warmth at night.

A pond can border the patio in a straight or curved line. Large ponds offer the possibility of making the patio stand out, rectangular or curving, like a stage above the pond surface, so that one has a varied view of it and gets the impression of being surrounded by water.

Above all, one must think of water's nighttime magic, with its reflections and sparkling effects. Tasteful lighting conjures it, swimming balls of light, rays that stretch almost horizontally across the surface, or spotlights that artistically illuminate the shrubs or bushes on the shore from below. Underwater lights, too, following the jets of fountains, achieve exotic effects.

When there is not enough space for a pond, there still remain many alluring ways to bring water to the patio. You may consider whether you want to enliven the patio with the splashing and murmuring of moving water, or you may give preference to the meditative reflections of standing water: in the form of basins (raised or sunken into the ground) channels, and tubs. If they are enlivened with sprays or water bells, they take on, like rapids or small waterfalls, their own lives as constant sources of sound.

This fragrant seat beside roses and bellflowers inspires one to dream. A nostalgic wire trellis in the form of a baroque pyramid and the floral cushion add to the romantic mood with their color, shape, and material.

Decorative Accessories and Containers

Surrounded by beautiful objects, one feels good, for they inspire the senses, raise the quality of life, and share their spirit with one's personal lifestyle. This is true both indoors and outdoors, thus also for the patio. It is not a piling-up of many *objets d'art*, but rather a few permanent fixtures that add stylish accents. Beginning with the beloved rose balls that refreshingly contrast or emphasize the colors of the garden's flowers, it goes on to include pinecones and sculptures. All of them contribute to the flair of the patio, whether Mediterranean, rustic, playfully romantic, or realistically modern.

This enhanced creation begins with useful amenities that should complement the overall style and taste of the patio. These include fixed lights, as well as moving lights and wind lights, plant supports and trellis elements, but also textiles and the dishes used on the patio.

Much importance belongs to the plant containers, in which the appearance of a plant is staged impressively, depending on whether it is in a flat or high container, on the ground, or in a raised site. The character of the container's material can also complement the appearance of a plant, and is often part of a style trend, whether terracotta, ceramic, lead, iron with rusty patina, fiberglass cement, steel, plastic, or wood.

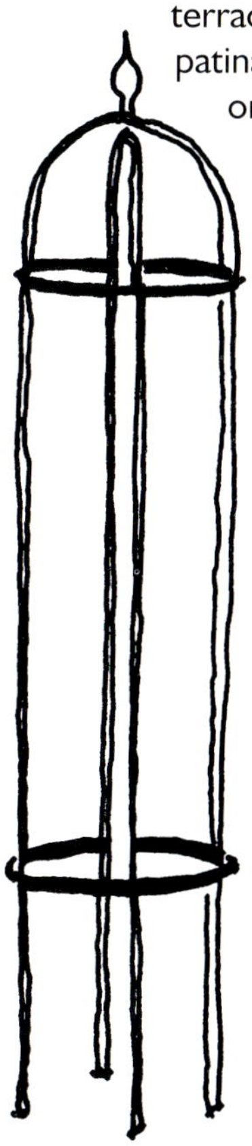

Trellis obelisks made of steel pipe are attractive vertical elements for beds bordering the patio. For potted-plant gardens there are decorative pendants to put up on the pots or insert into the substratum.

Busts and other ornaments effect a poetic blend with potted plants and bring them into one's field of vision. If they resist frost, they can also unfold their magic on the patio in winter.

Elegant bowls and columns can turn unspectacular plants into eye-catchers. They form material accents at the transition from the patio to the garden, but two of them can also serve as a formal gateway into it.

Creative Ideas for Small Patios

It is the same as with small gardens: The smaller the available area is, the more carefully it has to be laid out, for in small spaces, conceptual incongruities and errors become noticeable very quickly and clearly.

Optimal Surface Use

Small patios should, if possible, be rectangular, as this shape allows for more efficient use of space. Patio owners should decide what kind of outdoor seating they want the patio to accomodate, since multiple uses are usually impossible to achieve with limited space.

If the patio borders the garden, the sitting area can be extended into the garden. Whoever does not want to make this effort can help the cause with an appropriate garden layout. The garden beds can be turned sideways or moved in one direction up to the patio, so that if necessary, the sitting area can be extended onto the grass on the other side. A patio that gives way smoothly to the lawn on at least one side gives the impression of more space. If this is wanted, the patio should not be surrounded with shrubbery or walls.

For small patios on a slope, there is the possibility of planting shrubs or extending the patio on posts, like a stage over the sloping garden. A gentle slope can be handled with tall, connecting step-like decks, or a second patio linked to the first by a landing or stairs. When the ground slopes upward, the slope can be excavated for a large patio and enclosed by steps and walls, which can then function as comfortable places to sit.

This small roof patio comes alive with striking chairs and unified color, with the flooring under it as a quiet ground.

The Art of Optical Illusions

Small patios look bigger when small-sized materials such as bricks, patio blocks, small stone, or mosaic pavement are used to construct them. The smaller the material, the thinner the cracks should be. Laying the pieces in regular order awakens the impression of rest and distance, which is then enhanced when the material of the adjoining living space continues onto the patio. Perspective effects can also be achieved with the structuring of the pavement. Wooden planks or strips laid crosswise make surfaces look wider and shorter; laid lengthwise, they look narrower and longer. Many patterns, like herringbone and Dutch designs, enlarge small patios visually when they are laid diagonally, for then they lead the eye to the outside.

Here the slight slope has enlarged the patio surface, with the extension matching the level of the garden. Noble elegance and expansiveness are exuded by the uniform wood planking, turning the floor and edges into a bowl. At the same time, any number of sitting or lying places are created.

Danish furniture in summer white crowns the small sitting area in the green jungle of this patio. Although its design looks large-scale, thanks to its color and transparency it looks light and is integrated harmoniously.

Unbounded Living Culture

Luckily, among the many types of patio furniture there exist many options for creating a tiny paradise with luxuries that afford comfort and beauty in a small amount of space. Even with small patios, one need not do without outdoor hospitality when the choosing of tables and chairs is oriented to specific criteria.

The First Principle is Flexibility

In exceptional situations one can crowd somewhat closer together on a small patio. For everyday use, though, a comfortable extent of mobility must be preserved. Thus, there are certain requirements the furnishings must meet: Tables and chairs should be lightweight, so that if need be, one can move them easily from inside to outside. Even better: Chairs that can be folded or stacked and tables that can be moved out or folded up. Whoever wants or needs to save more space can choose square tables instead of round or oval ones, since seating around them takes up a little less space, as do chairs without arms. One can save even more space by choosing benches instead of chairs and set up the table with one side against the house or wall.

Awnings, marquees, and pergolas also take up no space while shading the patio, and are thus preferable to freestanding sunshades.

Color and Pleasant Shapes

The bigger chairs and tables look on small patios, the lighter and softer their colors should be. On the other hand, iron filigree furniture can have stronger and darker colors and yet look delicate. Heavy massive wooden furniture that gives a very weighty impression, and extensive basket chairs are not for small patios, nor are multicolored gatherings of furniture.

Strong colors do not belong on light furniture. The uniform background and flooring prevent disturbance caused by confusing mixtures of color.

The table can be unfolded to serve as a festive board. The unity of deck and furniture helps the sizeable chairs fit in.

Benches that lean against the wall need little space but offer plenty of seating. An arched rosebush and climbing vines create a magical garden effect.

Flower Power at Airy Heights

Naturally, small patios should also be dreamy green refuges. To keep plants and furniture from competing for limited space on a small patio, the solution is to remove plants from the foot space and walkways, or at least limit their presence.

What sounds very theoretical is easy to accomplish with climbing vines that can clamber up walls and roofed pergolas. Mediterranean romanticism is created by grapevines planted before or beside the patio, sometimes growing across the entire patio along the house wall, and even under balcony overhangs. A bucolic scene develops in the autumn when the grapes dangle above the patio.

Naturally, the walls can also be used for etageres, leaning and standing shelves, atop which small green gardens of potted plants can reside.

Long-stemmed roses or potted plants exude fairytale charm while taking up little ground space, and with something planted at their feet the result is a sea of flowers on two levels.

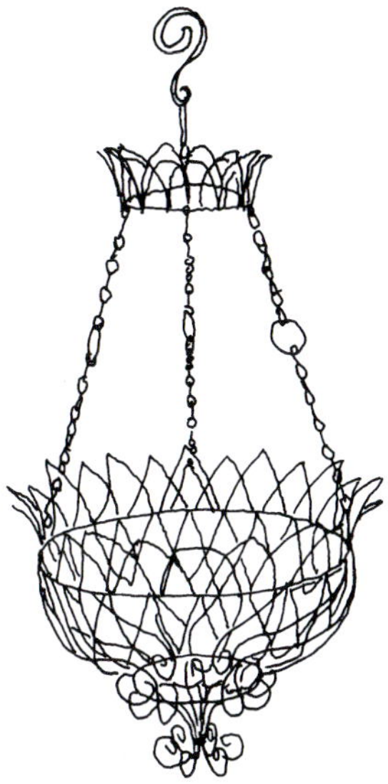

"Wirework," as the British call these handmade hangers of galvanized iron, enrich patios with the flair of the Victorian Age. Instead of plants, they can also contain wind lights or other decorations.

Ivy has already engulfed the small inside courtyard with enduring green. The shade-loving shrubs need no help for climbing, hanging firmly on the walls by their tendrils.

A similar effect can also be achieved with hanging plants in bowls or urns on pillars. Vertical cascades of green display their beautiful blossoms, just like hanging plants in pots that hang down from a wall, or let their flowery garlands flow down from metal containers or hanging baskets. The containers and flowers should be installed so that one will not bump into them, but so they will be easy to reach for care and watering. The chance of overflowing water running down the wall or onto the seats should also be avoided.

New Flowers for Hanging Pots and Baskets

—**Wishbone Flowers** (*Torenia fournieri)*
—**Pimpernel** (*Anagallis tenella)*
—**Golden Lobelia** (*Monopsis lutea)*
—**Hanging Snapdragons** (*Antirrhinum pendula multiflorum)*
—**Miniature Petunia 'Million Bells'**
—**Hanging Bamboo 'Green Twist'** (*Agrostis stolonifera)*
—**Yellow Petunia 'Lemon Plume'** (Tricolor *Petunia)*
—**Yerba Buena** (*Satureja douglasii)*

On small patios, too, nature can establish itself, as this cozy, shadowy place shows. Ivy and wild grapes let garlands and draperies flow down from airy heights, while ferns, mosses, Funkias, wild strawberries, and other shade plants in raised beds add to idle summer hours without impinging on the living and playing space.

Creative Ideas for Large Patios

Aristocratic patios often arise as transitional areas between stately buildings and equally stately gardens, thus radiating a particular harmony. But less extensive relaxation zones can also be enlarged. This may happen by extending their surface into the garden by laying them out around several sides of the house or developing them as garden courtyards. Large patios are strokes of luck and fulfill many of their owners' living dreams. However, one should not try to expand a sitting place between smaller buildings and gardens at the cost of suitable proportions.

Creating Seclusion

Broad, bare surfaces quickly take on a mood of desolation. Whether or not this happens to a patio depends less on its size in square feet than on its shape. On a large rectangular and over-seeable surface that may also lie above the garden, discomfort is more likely to be aroused than on a patio running around a corner with several centers, or an area that is organically linked with the garden and its plants through bulges and cutouts.

On large-scale undivided areas, though, even the nicest sitting place can seem lonesome if the splendid potential of this open area is not utilized. With just a few tricks it can be changed into worlds to withdraw into, in which private luxury is blended with a stylish and inspiring atmosphere.

—Tip 1: Give the patio a protective border. This job is done by enclosing walls, cut hedges, balustrades, beds, single shrubs, walls of vines and pergolas, and also by potted plants that line the patio edge in individual groups and thus turn away sight and wind simultaneously. These elements must not form either a unified or a hermetic belt around the patio. Just a few hints are enough to awaken an impression of protection. In forming the area around the patio, one should create axes of view into the garden rather than completely closing off the patio.

—Tip 2: Give the patio a protective roof. As already noted, pergolas, marquees, awnings, and parasols take over such jobs.

—Tip 3: Give the patio an internal frame. This means dividing the surface with elements that afford a feeling of space while creating separate areas within the same patio. These elements should offer comfort, aesthetics, and permanence. Hearths and grill locations, high beds and plant islands, or water basins and reflecting pools can perform such tasks.

The larger the garden and patio are, the higher protection-giving shrubs can be.

One does not notice the size of this patio, since the projecting border formation gives the impression that nature has gradually conquered a part of it. Its surface also seems less dominant because the adjacent pond with its varying surface attracts attention to itself.

A step as a cross line with a pump in the middle of it liven up the patio with interesting structures, even in winter when the furniture and potted plants are removed.

Manifold Areas of Use

The more objects placed on a patio, the more areas that form as a result. Each area created should be used according to the objects placed there. For instance, the area created by a brick-based grill that divides the patio should be used for eating rather than sunbathing. Conversely, the area next to a water basin or a colorfully blooming living sight screen, a sunbathing area fits very well. From here the garden can be observed while relaxing.

Living and Enjoying

Along with a sitting place for social gatherings and culinary enjoyment near the house, one should conceive of quiet, out-of-the-way areas for sunbathing and relaxing. The greatest swimming plea-

Tip

Order of Planning

—Make a list of desired uses.
—Then assign individual areas to them.
—Keep in mind where the sun will shine.
—Select suitable dividing elements.
—Conceive these so that they go with the house and patio in style, material, size, and color.

Such massive brick pillars for a glass-roofed pergola are only suitable for really large patios. Between the pillars, their concrete cores covered with bricks, there is room for various uses.

sure is promised by a pond that stretches out from the sitting place, or a pool that is integrated into the patio.

Grill chefs can set up a place with a masonry-mounted grill plus extensive counter and storage spaces.

Plants and Other Hobbies

The great variety of available plants will make the potting gardener's heart beat faster with the opportunity to promote their passion for plants with islands, high beds, and decorative basins.

Besides that, one can also enjoy many other hobbies on one's own patio areas. A fitness corner with appropriate equipment for exercising outdoors is just as possible as a dartboard corner or a table tennis area.

Places for Children to Play

One will want to know that small children are safely playing near the house, so as always to keep an eye on them. A lawn to crawl on can quickly give way to a sandbox or wading pool, which can be closed off by a safety fence or gate. Playing areas for building and making things as well as exercising are also possible on a patio.

Water Zones

Whether a high basin or a pond, brook, fountain, or sprayer, water on the patio can spoil patio owners with its attractions. Standing water offers magical views with sparkle and mirroring, while water in motion fills the patio with splashing and restful murmuring.

The individual use areas are clearly laid out on this modern patio. The sitting area near the house, the lying area with a view of the garden, plus a multipurpose high bed that offers varied attractions as a central space divider that offers additional seating for social gatherings.

Melodic splashing fills this patio when the transparent overflow from the high bed falls into the adjoining basin. A world of senses enlivened by water and plants is set in modern geometric architecture.

Important Equipment

Large patios absolutely need:
—Water sources. One can even place them at the outside wall of the house oneself; putting them under the patio or in the garden is an expert's job.
—Electric lighting, since candlelight is not safe enough for large patios.
—Water pipes that can be shut off to avoid burst pipes in winter.

A monolith full of character, this monumental table of natural stone attracts all eyes and can serve generations for celebrations and spare time. Its combination with aluminum chairs is extravagant.

Furnishing in All Sizes

Naturally, the furnishings of large patios should blend harmoniously.

Furniture

It can be large-dimensioned and weighty in form. Suitable in roofed areas is imposing rattan furniture, while classic massive wood furniture of enduring plantation teak is ideal in the open, for it livens up the patio with its shapes even in winter. "Space eaters" like artistic wooden couches, deck chairs, rockers, beach chairs, or hanging mats with their frames offer additional luxury and comfort.

Lighting

Large patios need electric light that affords a good view of distant areas. Steps, thresholds, and fixed installations, as well as entrances and exits should be well lit, as should the entire sitting area. One can make use of various sources of light. For example, it looks very interesting when spotlights illuminate parts of the planted border from below. Lights can be integrated into steps and pavements, creating a stone-like effect on the surface.

Useful and Luxurious Installations

Storage space for garden tools, pots, pillows, and other accessories is necessary. Containers or high beds with permanent plantings, such as water areas with natural stone troughs, fountain stones, or decorative basins, and even water-emitting sculptures divide the patio with charm.

Far Eastern inspiration is offered by this impressive pavement, which offers contrasts in various ways. The thin natural stone plates that transform smoothly into lines split the surface into irregular parcels. This dynamic large structure takes on tranquility from the filling of small pieces. The stones bedded in mortar are regular in every parcel, but laid in different directions.

Surface Design with Contrast

Large patios should not just pamper with luxury and relaxing comfort, but should also please the eye when not in use, enlivening the surface with interesting structure when bare of plants and furniture.

Space-Seeking Surfaces

So that large patios do not become boring, their surfaces should display striking patterns. They can be made of large paving stones or polygonal plates with large gaps laid out in decorative segments or sweeping curves. They can be made of two colors or two types of materials, but even bricks in herringbone or plaited patterns are suitable for such surfaces.

Colors, spots, and accents can also relax a large pavement. For example, colored mosaic stones or tiles, frost-resistant flagstones or assorted pieces, and lovingly scattered patterns of gravel can add interest to an expansive surface.

Plants also add to the surface decor. If grass or moss is allowed to grow in wide gaps, then regular or irregular carpet-like woven patterns of pavement and green plants soon develop. Self -seeding flowers that take hold in cracks, such as Lady's Mantle (*Alchemilla mollis*), Horned Violets (*Viola cornuta*), or Sweet Violets (*Viola odorata*) also look lovely. In small cutouts on sunny patios rock-garden bushes like fragrant Creeping Thyme (*Thymus serpillum*), Houseleek (*Sempervivium* hybrids), Wall Rock Cress (*Arabis caucasics),* or Cheddar Pink (*Dianthus gratianopolitanus*), can also be planted.

Attractive Eye-Catchers

The surfaces of large patios can be structured permanently not only horizontally, but can also offer the eye attractive variations with vertical accents. Eye-catchers should fit in with the ambience and be frost-resistant, so that they offer an artistic view even when covered with winter frost. Thus, solitary shrubs and trees planted in large cutouts in the patio pavement let one experience the changing seasons from indoors, and can herald the coming of Christmas with romantic strings of colored lights. Sculptures, winter-resistant containers, and other objects also afford accents that catch the eye.

The strongly structured, large-stone pavement of this patio with its striking gaps gives way to enclosed, sparkling surfaces of water in the ornamental basin and pond. Two objects direct the eye: the flower container in front and the white bench in the background.

Sitting Places in the Garden

Paradise Islands in the Green World

Time to relax amid light and shadow is afforded by seating in the midst of nature, allowing garden fans to enjoy their work with pride.

Models of Comfort

Unlike a patio beside the house, a sitting area in the garden indulges you with an alternative program of charm and comfort. If the patio is set up primarily for appearance and socializing, one can doubly treasure a quiet, out-of-the way place amid humming bees and fluttering butterflies. On the other hand, whoever has set up the patio as a private refuge may treasure a wild, romantic grill or fireplace in a corner of the garden far from the house for festivities with friends. These examples already show that sitting places offer a broad spectrum of possibilities.

With all the variety, there are criteria that lend every sitting place a homey character and generate good feelings, imbed it in the fragrant world of plants, and at the same time, make it an artistic ornament in the garden.

—Its location should be selected so that it offers new views of the house and garden. While seats in formal gardens are situated eye-catchingly in a central location or at the end of paths and axes of view, in free-form gardens they can also be hidden away in cozy corners. But it is always important that the view there offers special attractions or rewarding changes. For this reason, a seat can always be situated by a pond or brook.

—The seat itself should protect one's back. This protection from the rear can be given by the most varied elements such as walls, fences, or trellises that appear all the more natural when they are covered by green vines. One can also entrust this job to taller plants such as hedges, shrubs, trees, or high bushes.

—These places more completely become relaxing refuges when they also offer lateral protection. Niches in hedges, walls, or beds respond to this primal need. In formal gardens one gets by with freestanding benches and evergreen shrubs that can be wrapped around them like a green collar and trimmed to shape.

—Finally, the sitting place itself, with its surface and furnishings should also offer a nice view from a distance. Its arrangement and pavement contribute to this just as its furniture and accessories do. Flowers in chic boxes, tall trunks flanking it on both sides, and a decorative arch of roses over a bench are effective.

Here the view is arranged reciprocally. From the ornamental sitting place one looks across beds of flowers and greens to the artistic gazebo, which in turn affords a view of the seat.

Fixed Seats for Socializing

By fixed seats one means those located permanently on a firm foundation, on which the furniture stands safely and one can sit securely. Often-used surfaces in particular should have a frost-safe and skid-safe foundation of paving stones or slabs, since expanses of grass cannot withstand such use for long. As a rule, paved walkways lead to these sitting places, and these paths should blend with the material and arrangement of the seating, especially in a small garden.

Size of the Surface

The dimensions of the plot depend on the plans for its use and the spatial conditions of the garden. For a group of chairs or lounges they must be larger than for one bench. Whoever has the option should go beyond the needed space in order to include useful storage space, plants, and decorative accessories.

The Shape of the Seating

Fixed sitting places form striking elements in the garden area through their shape and surface material, for they divide the area horizontally and on the surface without furniture or bordering plants. Thus they create effects that should not be undervalued, and can be included deliberately as decorative formative elements.

Rectangular surfaces generally blend into the garden unobtrusively. When choosing the pavement, one is not limited and can select large plates just as well as a pavement of small components. Such sitting places have a particularly harmonious effect when the table repeats the shape of the ground area.

Round surfaces have a centering power and immediately draw attention to themselves. In this case, small types of pavement are appropriate, as they can more easily be used to create a circular shape. A round table reinforces the quiet charm of these sitting places.

In a rectangular courtyard with a square decorative basin, the scenic seating provides an unconventional looseness.

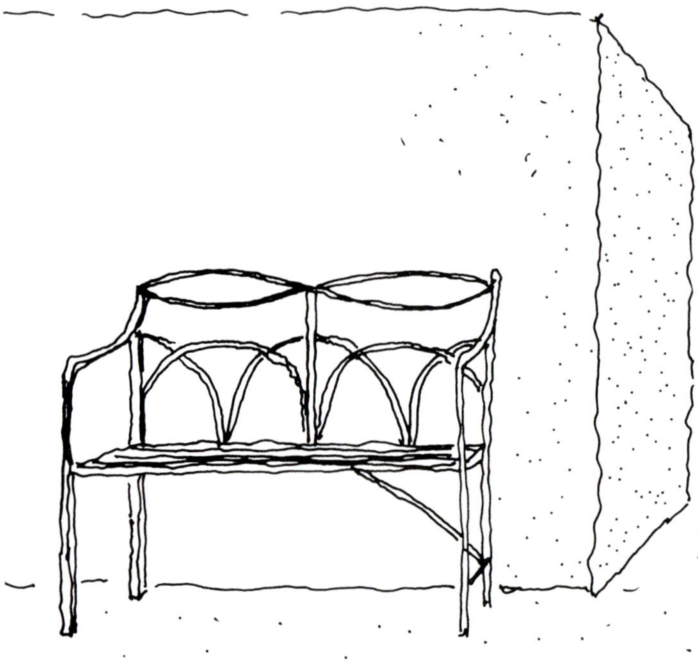

The round brick pavement of this seating place contrasts clearly with the lawn and forms a magical circle before the background of humorous and fantastic animal figures.

This elegant wrought-iron bench is a classic of English garden art. Its graceful original stands in the world-renowned Hidcote Manor Garden and orients itself to models of the Regency style from the late 18th and early 19th centuries.

Thus one can calculate needed space

The smallest area of a sitting place can be reckoned by the following rules:
—Length of the table plus 2 meters (for chairs and room to move), times
—Width of the table plus 2 meters (for chairs and room to move)
—Important: Voluminous furniture takes up more space.
—Important: Round tables need more space than rectangular ones.

The wide, enclosing walls of this small, round alcove in slightly rising terrain can also serve as seating, where day lilies stand near to offer their charm and fragrance.

This sitting place on a hanging patio also looks very idyllic from above. Wreathed in heat-absorbing walls and the luxuriant green of surrounding shrubs, it offers an artistic view into the valley beyond.

The Garden Situation

In formal gardens, seating is a definitive part of the architectural formation, with the task of catching the eye in the middle of path intersections or at the end of aisles and paths – often in front of sculptured hedges. In free-form gardens they can also be hidden away cozily. If they are at the same height as the garden, they can easily be turned into places of unforgettable garden pleasure with the addition of fragrant, blossoming plants.

Sunken Seating

If the sitting area is lower than the surrounding garden, it takes on an incomparable flair of privacy and sensory intensity. Such special places can be placed on terraced slopes or in a classic sunken garden. For these bordered medallion forms, one can select an area of desired size in a garden and adorn the bottom with a water basin, at whose rim the sitting place promises varied experiences. The framing wall crowns can be planted with fragrant, soft, and hanging shrubs, which one can enjoy at an unusual eye level thanks to the deeper level of the sitting place. In such deeply situated sitting places one is shielded from wind and sight. Here in changing seasons or evenings one can enjoy the warm air absorbed by stones and water during the day long into the night in the low spot.

But on a slope too, straight or semicircular cutouts form plateaus for sitting places, with the slope held back by walls or palisades.

Deeper seating offers the sitter views of particular penetration, whether he sees the plants from below or at eye level. Whoever builds dry walls to support the slope can plant their gaps charmingly and soon see how they develop into richly varied biotopes.

The form of this raised sitting place on the circular terrace plays with diverse rounded shapes: trimmed shrubs that are at once eye-catchers and green wreathing, surfaces, steps, and round-bellied pots.

This slightly raised rectangular sitting place is laid out like a stage and offers a view from above. A low, enclosing wall and a thick roof of tree leaves in the background offer visual seclusion.

Raised Seating

Situated on uneven ground or slopes, raised seats offer a pleasant extended view, but little privacy unless they are shielded from sight and wind. This can be achieved by pergolas with vine trellises or by robust shrubs that defy the winds that blow strongly in such places. In formal gardens they are sometimes dispensed with when the sitting place is more an eye-catcher than a relaxing refuge.

Formative Elements of Sunken Gardens

—The depth should add up to 80 to 160 centimeters.

—The center can also be accented with a flowerbed, statue, sundial, etc.

—Decorative steps offer the necessary access.

—Enclosing walls in stages allow flowerbeds with particularly lavish floral decoration serving as planted frames.

Mobile Seating for the Moment

These seats are not the result of a well thought-out and designed formation, but rather arise from a short-term necessity to dive into nature – surrounded by fluttering butterflies, and hummed at by swarms of busy bees. Above all, though, these flexible visits in the garden allow us to follow the course of the seasons and their fleeting attractions.

Refreshing breezes and cool shadows are afforded by a sitting place under tall trees. Folding chairs are practical to transport, even when they can stand in the rain like this teak set.

Celebrating and Enjoying With Friends

Who hasn't experienced the sudden realization that there are more visitors than the patio will hold? How nice when a long table on the lawn can then be conjured up to blend the relaxed atmosphere of happy socializing with the luxury of feasting amid the outdoor joys of life. Children's parties can also be great fun on the lawn. The danger of injury from merry bouncing around is much less on the lawn's green floor than on pavement, and if something falls from a plate or is spilled, the lawn gladly laps it up. Whoever feels too hot on his high patio at the height of the summer can enjoy his tea or coffee by moving beneath the wide crown of a shady tree.

For greater events and social occasions, one will generally expand onto the lawn. Of course, this should not happen regularly or constantly so the green carpet has a chance to survive. Whoever does not want to rule out such use of his lawn from the start should select a useful family lawn grass. These robust grasses are suitable for extraordinary seating and picnic areas. They do not suffer so much when children roll around on them. A solid program of maintenance stabilizes the useful green, which should be kept at a height of 1 to 2 inches with regular mowing and should be fertilized twice a year, in April and June.

Whether play space or picnic spot – life is pleasant in soft green surrounded by flowers.

Feather light loom chairs are not only available in various forms, but their charming elegance fits splendidly into modern ambiance. They should not, though, be exposed to the elements for long periods.

A white seasonal sitting place full of romantic impressions. In May the apple tree works magic with its splendid blossoms, while the green leaves of summer give refreshing shade. And in autumn, fresh juicy apples are near at hand to enjoy as if in a fairyland.

A romantic, fragrant seat under rambling roses.

In the hammock one can dream away whole summer days.

These comfortable lounges not only have adjustable backs, but also variable knee support. Thanks to their wheels, they are easily moved to any desired new location.

A deck chair of plantation teak can enrich garden parties all year with eye-catching nostalgic flair.

Quiet Hours for Relaxing

Whoever wants to escape from everyday life now and then to let his spirit swing between daydreams and nature, or immerse himself pleasantly in a book will particularly treasure a spot for himself alone. No permanent sitting place is necessary for this, for the whole garden with its seasonal high points offers new attractions again and again, which one can follow with a mobile seat according to his mood.

Variation is guaranteed. Suitable seats include armchairs, benches, chairs, and even a large stone, an accommodating root, or a tree stump in a natural garden can invite one for an idyllic visit. Lounges, deck chairs, and recliners let you put your feet up and take the sun, and if necessary, a few soft cushions on a wall will do. Hammocks stretched between two mighty trees, or a weather-resistant glider or rocker enchant, seeming for a time to lift one's inertia and lure one into an excursion through the realm of fantasy.

Seating places of this kind should be screened off. They are intimate places in which time seems to stand still, places that inspire a desire to meditate. They are thus not conceived as eye-catchers visible from afar, yet lovely modern or nostalgic furniture can blend well with their style and enhance it.

It is important to be able to experience the garden with all one's senses. One will want to choose a seat among roses or under a blossoming shrub, where one can revel in color and scent. Water also opens its own world to the senses. Whoever sits there in peace cannot avoid the magic of its gleaming surface, the reflections, and "water music." Besides, it is alluring when another biotope such as dry walls, wild shrubbery, or flowered meadows offer a colorful wealth of living things that one can sit still and enjoy watching.

Painted Metal

This flower ensemble proves that fantasy is an extensive land. In joyful creativity, thick sheet iron was welded into a flowery seat, merrily painted, and treated to resist the weather.

Carved Wood

Whether from the flea market or the gallery, chairs like this little shabby-looking throne orient themselves to various styles and techniques, and can set effective accents in a garden.

High-quality porch swings of plantation teak offer swinging good times in the garden all year round.

Furniture as Curiosities

Whether fixed in place or mobile, single seats do not merely enrich the garden with their comfort. Through special designs and colors they can also stress its style, contrast it, or fill it with extravagant life-like ornamental sculpture.

Originals by an Artist's Hand

Garden fans have a vast choice from a gigantic palette of creative seating, whether Victorian copies of cast iron or modern designer furniture. Before buying, one should not only check their appearance and comfort, but also their resistance to weather. To call truly singular garden furniture one's own requires much more researching of real *objets d'art* than choosing from a catalog. So why not let your own fantasies become realities?

Products of Personal Fantasy

With little effort and cost one can accomplish a remarkable lot. An old, worn-out kitchen chair often spends its declining years sadly in a storeroom. Treated with sensitivity and humor, it can glow in newfound splendor. Before one sets out to reform it, one should consider its future place in the garden and be sure its style and color will fit in.
—Wooden chairs can take on a new appearance in many ways with a new coat of paint in one or more colors, with soft or loud color accents. Patterns and regular decorations are best applied with a stencil. Wooden molding, carving, and roots can also give it a new life. The roots of an old tree that can no longer survive or gives too much shade can be turned into a natural seat with an appealing top panel and decorative carving.

Fiberglass This weather-resistant club chair is modeled after French terracotta. Several layers of fiberglass allow the comfortable armchair to resist many a rain shower.

Tile Mosaic This "comfortable" sofa may be indestructible, with its concrete body resting on a frost-secure foundation. Small tiles have been glazed and applied in colorful mixtures.

Plastic As small pink sculptures, these Italian designer chairs liven up a small inside courtyard with futuristic charm – even if they aren't used for sitting.

—In prepared wooden frames, simple cement shapes can be cast to be colored or fitted playfully into stonework, irregular pieces, or mosaics. Finished hollow blocks of stone can also be polished and decorated in various ways.

—Artistic chairs can be welded together out of old metal from the junkyard or flea market. Welding courses that steadily grow in popularity show how popular this work has become. Granted, rusty chairs do not suit everyone, but they fit very nicely into the garden world, especially when combined with terracotta elements. Stable wire weaves are also suitable for playful metalwork. Welded or wired into spheres or cubes to be filled with stones and topped off with a nice wooden or stone seat, they form very unique seats for minimalist modern gardens.

Colors and Shapes

Whoever is creatively active cannot underestimate the influence of colors. The smaller the garden is, the more carefully one should apply strong colors; it is better to limit yourself to two or three colors. An original single seat surrounded by peaceful green can function as a lively eye-catcher anywhere. Bright or pastel-colored flowerbeds would naturally compete with its effect. Wood, earth, rust tones, and green subordinate themselves with restraint to the plant world. White, black, and blue, on the other hand, are classic accenting colors along with red and metallic gray. But it is worthwhile to experiment at times, for even violet or yellow seats look good in suitable surroundings.

The flair of Colonial style flows from this decorative Indonesian bench. But the classic repertoire of benches made of plantation teak, oak, and robinia is also weather-resistant.

This rustic bamboo bench not only invites social togetherness, but also gives plants a place for a rendezvous. A delicate white finish makes it an effective eye-catcher.

White wooden benches are definite eye-catchers and should always be placed as such, for example, at the end of wooded walks and paths, before trimmed hedges or under tall trees.

This curved stone bench blends perfectly into the ensemble of the paved circle. It does not direct the gaze into the garden, but toward the richly planted urn that stands in the center of the circle.

Formally formed, this curved stone bench still has a natural effect, with the green walls of the boxwood hedge guaranteeing a well-proportioned air of cozy companionship.

This teak bench owes its silver-gray patina to wind and weather. The stone guardian gives it protection and attracts notice. In formal gardens, benches are often flanked on both sides.

The Fluidity of Lovely Benches

Although the climate does not always invite us to sit outdoors in England, benches became a central formative element there, where no large garden was complete without them. In the whole of Great Britain a tradition of a dozen models took shape; they were copied for years, and thanks to their classic beauty, they have come to possess the rank and function of sculptures.

Stone benches and copies of frost-resistant cast concrete spotted with moss or mildew blend into the garden artistically, even though they are usually cold and uncomfortable. Models with decorative flutings or lions' heads often go back to Italian patterns and have a fine stylistic effect.

Modern examples made of large stone slabs look massive and require a lot of space around them. One should limit them to large gardens.

Wooden benches, depending on their style and color, can look rustic or elegant. Finely worked white benches look good in city gardens, even small ones, while big massive wooden benches, whether straight or semicircular, go well in larger free-form or natural gardens.

Metal benches show a Mediterranean flair, elegant nobility, or romantic lightheartedness. Whether wrought or cast iron, most of them are treated to be relatively long lasting. Painted black with filigree work, they are especially decorative and go well in even the smallest garden. Made of new materials such as steel and aluminum, they usually have a functional design that destines them for modern gardens.

Benches can also originate from splendid playfulness. Niches in retaining walls on slopes can be bridged with a board to form a protected seat. High beds of airy flowers or herbs on stone walls can be enriched with an integrated step by a bench, while a climbing arch of roses over a bench can crown it with a Sleeping Beauty's grove.

Imaginative Seating for Two

Patios can't grant every wish. What is lacking may be offered by a quiet refuge in the garden. Sitting places fill the garden with life and offer family members the most varying places to get away from it all. Above all, they let the garden be experienced close-up in all its manifold facets.

One can never have enough places to sit. Whoever is thinking of setting up a second, third, or fourth one should not lose sight of two aspects:
—The seat should offer alternatives to the patio
—It should possess its own charm and experience.

Sitting places show the house and garden from other points of view. They also enrich the green paradise with new attractions. The more impressions and changing charms such a place offers, the larger it appears. And for those who use the sitting place, new things keep moving into the realm of sensory awareness. Thus, small all-year sitting places which one seeks out especially at the high point of their vegetation are rewarding: the spring seat under a blooming apple tree or lilac bush, the summer seat amid fragrant roses, or the autumn seat when the grasses color their splendid fountains.

By installing a sitting place, one also increases the garden's variety. A dark corner no longer needs to lie forsaken, becoming a shaded seat with its own charming flowers. A small pond affords the eye new hours-long voyages of discovery, and lets the quiet observer experience the changing seasons from a new viewpoint. A seat in a vegetable garden, on the other hand, allows the healthy splendor to ripen with the gardener's pride or be picked fresh and cleaned on the spot.

Second or third seats need not be the same size or always offer seats to a group; one chair or bench is usually enough. It is worthwhile to examine the garden from the standpoint of new locations for seats. Every spot in the garden not only has new light conditions, but also ground qualities that invite a different planting. If the ground in front of a south-facing patio is light and dry, it may be heavier and damp in a low spot of a shady corner, and thus be home to a completely different society of plants. Thus the planting around the seat surely increases the variety of plants in the garden and lures many animal guests in.

A low spot in a garden offers itself as a place for a cozy group of seats.

Nowhere can pleasant summer evenings be enjoyed in more idyllic style than on a spare-time patio facing westward.

White furniture makes dark places glow from inside so that even somewhat dark-colored flowers gain. Here, fuchsias grow in the shadows; their cheery blossoms go well with the decorative furniture.

Pleasant Seating in the Shade

A romantic little spot under a tall tree or before a bewitching shrub coulisse will probably be the patio owner's first place of refuge in the garden. Here he can stand the heat of midsummer, for the surrounding shrubbery exudes refreshing coolness.

Such a place deserves to be treasured as a jewel. Shadowy sitting places should offer a stable surface, since dampness will last unusually long there for lack of sun and warmth. For this reason, one should not select a wooden surface, which would become slippery with dampness and quickly attract algae. A light surface of pavement or slabs conjures up friendliness in the gloomy shadows. The ornamental alternative is a dark surface with a large-scale inlaid mosaic, perhaps with sun, moon, stars, or spirals.

For furniture and plants the watchword is: choose white or pastel shades. If the place cannot be planted because there are too many roots running through it, one can make do with shrubs and bushes in pots. In large pots White Hortensia (*Hydrangea arborescens*), Rhododendron (*Rhododendron* hybrids), Yew (*Taxus baccata*), Ivy (*Hedera helix*), and Boxwood (*Buxus sempervirens*) will thrive, as will a number of pleasant shade-giving shrubs.

Shade-giving Shrubs for Potting

—**Lady's Mantle** (Alchemilla mollis)
—**Funkia** (Hosta hybrids)
—**Saxifrage** (Bergenia hybrids)
—**Saxifrage** (Saxifraga hybrids)
—**Alumroot** (Heuchera hybrids)
—**False Spiraea** (Astilbe hybrids)
—**Deadnettle** (Lamium maculatum)
—**Great Bellflower** (Campanula latifolia var. macrantha)

High hedges and shrubs throw long shadows. A bright bench provides visual relaxation, refreshing coolness on a hot day, and a pleasant view of blooming beds in moving sunshine.

Bright sculptures can do away with the doubtful shadow-life of dark garden areas by attracting and capturing the gaze with their expressive power. Reflecting rose balls also catch a little light and hang onto it.

This shadowy spot has an almost bowerlike character. Its approach, which the sun's rays reach, brightly directs the view into the open with the lively Bush Cinquefoil (*Potentilla fruticosa*) and colorful flowers.

Before this inspiring shadowed place, a meadow of Marguerite shows its loveliest side. A path of steppingstones crosses it cautiously, widening into a defined surface at the sitting place.

Located in a far corner of the garden, this shadowy sitting place reveals the green paradise from a new viewpoint. A picturesque old tree with ivy ascending its trunk provides back cover and shade.

Idylls at the Edge of the Garden

Particularly in small gardens that are thoroughly formed, one usually cannot locate a sitting place within the garden space, but only on its edges. This need not be a disadvantage if one upgrades a far place into a cheerful domicile.

Using the Border

Depending on the circumstances, the border formation can be included in the sitting place.

—House, garage, and garden walls can protect the back of the sitting place. Of course, they should be brightened up with climbing plants. Recommended for shadowy places are evergreen English Ivy (*Hedera helix*) and Climbing Hydrangea (*Hydrangea anomala* ssp. *petiolaris*), which can climb walls without help. If little space is available, a folding wooden bench can be attached to, or a wall bench be built into the wall.

—Before free-growing or trimmed hedges, the sitting place should keep a bit of distance so that the green walls can be maintained and trimmed.

—Sight screening should be provided in the case of low walls and plantings. Walls of vines or palisades take up the least space, and the latter can be made part of the green garden with climbing vines.

All of these places can be seen from above by near neighbors. In this case, a wide vine trellis and climbing shrubs should be used to turn the bench area into a bower. A tree with a crown that shuts off the view from above becomes a very natural sightscreen. Until it has grown to the required size, a large sunshade can provide worthy service.

These sites should include artistic plantings that attract one to them. This also links them with the garden, into which the view is cleverly directed by accents, paths, frames, or aisles.

Joy in small things is expressed in this seat cuddling close to a wall. The bench is romantically framed by an arching rosebush, whose glowing red blossoms fill the little refuge with intoxicating fragrance. The matching floral tablecloth shows that textiles can also be used to add color to sitting places.

A fence of thick rails defines the boundary of the yard and allows climbing plants like the lovely-leaved Dutchman's Pipe (*Aristolichia macrophylla*), as well as Russian Vine and roses, to ascend it. A picturesque tree turns sun and sight away, while beautiful blossoms like bellflowers spread from the gaps in the pavement.

This formation plays with surface contrasts, opposing the green boundary of the garden wall with the circle of the sitting place.

Intimate Garden Spaces

Remember that secret hiding place of childhood, into which you withdrew with worries or a favorite book, in which you indulged in dreams and plans, undisturbed and unfindable by the world – who would not want to take something of that place with them into adult life!

In the garden one can reclaim a little of that – with an isolated sitting place that makes lovely dreams come true. One can go there and read fiction, another can meditate, a third can immerse himself in nature, while a fourth could have a nice little open-air bar or sculpture gallery.

Whatever brings joy is allowed in laying out an intimate garden space. Furniture, accessories, colors, and plants are selected according to an individual's wishes and interests, not those of the whole family. As in the furnishing of a room, one will also adorn this place with things that bring back special memories, or to which one feels especially drawn. They can be objects found in nature such as stones or roots, just as well as plants, art, or cult objects, or things that capture a mood and give the sitting place a special flair.

Those who enjoy gardens will also find this pleasure in places where the garden shows itself, in certain seasons, from its best side. For example, under a blossoming canopy of climbing roses, or at an autumn seat amid red-gold leaves. Nature lovers can set up a small seat very close to a biotope where they can watch birds raise their brood, lizards sit on dry walls, or dragonflies and frogs play by a pond. And what whirring, rustling, and fluttering can be perceived when one sits very still in the midst of a spicily fragrant herb garden.

It pays to attend to details in making a sitting place. Noble plant supports can do the same job as bamboo stakes, but spread a more evocative atmosphere.

In the autumn a garden gives a last show of its ability to change. Reason enough to watch, enveloped in a soft, snug woolen blanket, as the maple changes into the colors of a sunset, and revel in the flowers and fruits of the changing season.

A sunken spot, splendid for undisturbed reading.

An espresso place for a quick fill-up.

Time seems to stand still in this oasis.

This romantic spot in the shade tells of elfin joys and flowers in May, with the ornamental leaves of Lady's Mantle (*Alchemilla mollis*), Ostrich Fern (*Matteuccia struthiopteris*), and Funkia (*Hosta* hybrids), and the shy flower faces of Columbines (*Aquilegia* hybrids), and behind them the buds of Chinese Peonies (*Paeonia lactiflora* hybrids) promising still more imposing splendor.

Plant Name	Location	Blooms	Height	Water	Care
Cheddar Pink *Dianthus gratianopolitanus* (bush)	sunny	May to July	2-8in. (5-20cm)	moderate, no puddles	trim after blooming
Day Lily (fragrant) *Hemerocallis hybrids* (bush)	sunny to part shade	May to September	12-45in. (30-120cm)	slightly moist ground	remove flowers after blooming
Sweet Pea *Lathyrus odoratus* (summer flower)	sunny to part shade	July to September	3-6ft. (1-2m)	moderately moist ground	shorten ends about 1/3
Lavender *Lavandula angustifolia* (small shrub)	sunny	June to August	12-32in. (30-80cm)	moderately dry ground	cut back in spring
Madonna & Regal Lily *Lilium candale, regale* (bulb flowers)	sunny, warm	June to July	30-55in. (80-150cm)	moderate, no puddles	support, cover in winter
Sweet Alyssum *Lobularia maritime* (summer flower)	sunny to part shade	May to October	2-6in. (5-15cm)	moderately moist ground	cut back after blooming
Honeysuckle *Lonicera periclymenum* (climbing vine)	sunny to part shade	July to August	9-15ft. (3-5m)	no matter	needs help climbing
Money Plant *Lunaria annua* (summer flower)	sunny to part shade	May to June	20-45in. (40-120cm)	slightly moist	seed in June, biennial
Stock *Matthiola incana* (summer flower)	sunny	June to August	12-35in. (30-100cm)	slightly, no puddles	support high varieties
Daffodil Varieties *Narcissus jonquila, N. tazetta, N. pooeticus*(bulb flowers)	sunny to part shade	April to May	8-20in. (20-50cm)	slightly, no puddles	trim only after yellowing
Mock Orange *Philadelphus hybrids* (shrub)	sunny to part shade	May to June	3-9ft. (1-3 m)	moderately moist ground	thin every 2-3 years
Garden Mignonette *Reseda odorata* (summer flower)	sunny	July to September	8-24in. (20-60cm)	slightly, no puddles	don't plant near roses
Roses (fragrant) *Rosa* varieties (small shrubs)	sunny	June to October	4in.-24 ft. (10cm-8m)	slightly, no puddles	remove flowers after blooming
Lilac *Syringa vulgaris* hybrids (shrub)	sunny	May to June	12-18ft. (4-6m)	slightly, no puddles	remove sprays after blooming
Fragrant Viburnum *Viburnum farreri* (shrub)	sunny to part shade	Nov/Dec to Feb/March	6-9ft. (2-3m)	moderately moist ground	thin every 2-3 years
Wisteria *Wisteria floribunda* (climbing vine)	sunny	May to June	18-30ft. (6-10m)	slightly moist ground	needs help climbing

The way to this rosy sitting place is itself a small surprise for the senses. While stately Peonies (*Paeonia lactiflora* hybrids) make their presence known with imposing blossoms to the right, gentle Bellflowers (*Campanula*) bow to the visitor on the left.

Luxuriant Flowers and Fragrances

What more could every day offer in the background than a seat with waves of flowers that not only lure with splendid colors, but find their way directly to your soul with their sweet, intoxicating fragrance? Whoever wants a little dreamland of the senses should reserve as sunny a place for it as possible, for many fragrant plants love the light. When this prerequisite is fulfilled, the whole world of plants offers flowers with enchanting perfumes from spring to autumn.

Fragrant shrubs or climbing vines can exude their aromas at nose level when they frame a sitting place, while a potpourri of good-smelling flowers enchants you in front of it. When planting is not possible, the senses can be satisfied with fragrant balcony and potted plants such as Datura (*Brugmansia* hybrids), Lemon-scented Verbena (*Aloysia triphylla*), citrus plants, Geraniums, or Heliotrope (*Heliotropium arborescens*). Many fragrant plants begin to release their extravagant perfumes more strongly only as night falls, so that some (like Datura or Regal Lilies) can even bring on headaches in sensitive "creatures of the night" with the heavy, almost Oriental opulence of their aromas.

Choosing a Color Scheme

Colors enhance the atmosphere of a sitting place and can serve as an emotional accent to evoke moods and effects. There are two possibilities: one can use the color of the furniture or its material as a formative means, and play with colors and designs of cushions, bolsters, and tablecloths. Since the latter can be exchanged, they allow color changes as one desires. Through uniform textiles, even colorfully gathered furniture appears to come from the same vat.

Colors enrich the garden, but one's use of them should be considered carefully. Here are a few tips:

—Dark garden areas take on color from bright furniture or fabrics.

—Select a maximum of three colors so that the sitting place does not become too jarring.

—The sitting place blends harmoniously into the garden when it picks up garden colors. They can be those of plants, containers, or garden decor.

—The sitting place that contrasts in color with its surroundings becomes a striking eye-catcher.

—Multicolored liveliness should be avoided in sitting furniture that takes up a large area. A single chair or bench, though, can liven up a dark corner and provide a lively accent.

—In natural gardens, natural colors blend better than more powerful ones. They can, though, enliven modern, formal, or free-form gardens.

—White garden furniture usually has an elegant or playful effect.

—Potted evergreen shrubs trimmed into geometrical shapes bring peace between all-too-colorful flowers in summer. In winter they serve as green sculptures, creating lively spots of color, and can even be decorated for Christmas.

This sitting place owes its overall impression of refreshing blue to its cushions and tablecloth. Without them, the likewise beautiful wood color would predominate.

This blue seating group has its effect through the color of the furniture and shows why blue is so popular. It forms a very intense contrast with the green of the plants.

This teak bench with its silver gray patina fits into the plant world splendidly. The green and white cushions pick up the colors of the peonies and leaves.

This teak bench with its silver gray patina fits into the plant world splendidly. The green and white cushions pick up the colors of the peonies and leaves.

This idyllic pond is reminiscent of a nymphaeum, with its mythical guardian exuding the magic of days long gone. In beautiful contrast to it is the modern white furniture, from which it is but a short step into the realm of fantasy.

Wooden deck, bridge, and teak furniture harmonize perfectly. At its edges, the plant world is allowed to enhance the seating, from which varying views are accented by sculpture.

Nicely integrated into the poolside plants is this sitting place with the Far Eastern mood of its basket furniture. The seat cushions repeat the color of the flowers on the pier.

Dolce Vita by the Water

No garden scene inspires relaxation as quickly as a sitting place by the water. That may be because water, an original element of life, exudes a mysterious allure. At the same time, it enchants and relaxes with its magical glitter, its murmuring and splashing, but also its fascinating plant and animal world.

Where there is water in the garden, there should be a place to sit, in addition to effective lighting that creates happy evening impressions.

Whether a natural pond, decorative basin, or brook, there can be sitting places beside water. Another situation arises when the sitting place resembles a raised stage that juts into the pond like a peninsula and thus guarantees an impressive view. These peninsulas are usually wooden decks, but can also be sitting or lounging places made from stone or pavement. The following combinations have proved themselves well:

—Natural pond with wooden deck and wooden furniture.

—Decorative basin surrounded by natural stone or plates that enliven the surface of the sitting place and its elegant furniture.

Sitting places by the water should be integrated into the plantings along the shore. Bamboo, Rhododendron, Hydrangea, and Snowball are just a few of the plants that look charming there and can create niche-like shields from the sides. The idyll becomes perfected all the more when luxuriant shoreline shrubbery is added. In large park-like gardens, solitary trees with overhanging "weeping" shapes create charming seats beside the water, where one sits under their branches as if in a bower.

Sitting and lying places on decks above the water appear bald and charmless if they are not accompanied by either taller plants from the garden or colorful, picturesque potted plants that link them with the garden and, arranged as small groups, suggest an optical frame.

This elegant seat by a decorative pond lets one feel something of the meditative peace and power of Asiatic gardens.

Trees and Shrubs to Sit Under

—**Weeping Birch** (*Betula pendula* "Tristis" or "Youngii")

—**European Beech** (*Fagus sylvatica* "Pendula" or "Purpurea Pendula")

—**European Ash** (*Fraxinus excelsior* "Pendula")

—**Crabapple** (*Malus* hybrid "Red Jade")

—**Japanese Cherry** (*Prunus serrulata* "Kiku-shidare-sakura")

—**Weeping Willow** (*Salix alba* "Tristis")

Bowers and Pavilions

Garden Cabins For Falling in Love

When trellises and plants create ornamental spaces in bowers and pavilions, they lure people into a realm of inspiration and relaxation, in which art and nature meet in the loveliest way.

Bowers – Floral Boudoirs for Romantics

Covered sitting places in the garden are high points of a green living culture. With a distinct mixture of plants and structures, they form shielded refuges full of magic and comfort. Within these small worlds of joy, open and closed designs can be differentiated and designated bowers, pavilions, garden houses, gazebos, and summerhouses. On the basis of their flowing transitions and varying appearance, they cannot always be defined precisely, and their names can often be swapped. In general though, bowers are understood to be outdoor sitting places under leaves, protected from sun and wind, with neither a solid roof nor fixed walls.

Architecture With Green Walls

Bowers, like no other garden element, lure their visitors into a transitional world of nature and architecture, where one sits in the midst of fragrant flowers and rustling walls of leaves. The more thickly the plants envelop the sitting place, the more coolness, moisture, and intimacy their foliage affords. It is no wonder that these wreathed retreats were once chosen as treasured and secret meeting places for a tender tryst.

Even today, bowers exude something of this nostalgic blessedness. In small gardens, faraway corners, or slim spaces, they can be used for enriching views and enhancing beauty. Depending on how they are built, they require little space and become enchanting special shapes, sitting places, and eye-catchers alike.

—Bedded in trellises, pergola elements, or arches of roses, benches become eye-catchers with the allure of a love-nest.

—Filigree forms in the shape of crossing arches of roses can hold a small group of seats, but can also arch over intersecting paths.

—Benches on both sides of a path spanned by a pergola have a long tradition as loveseats.

—Tree bowers, around which trees are planted in a semicircle or open form with interwoven crowns above the benches require more room. Thus branches can be made into veritable green igloos. But they should always have a high foundation built up with gravel or bark mulch to protect their root systems.

—Individual trees with screen-like hanging branches such as Scotch Elm (*Ulmus glabra* 'Camperdownii') or European Beeches (*Fagus sylvatica* 'Pendulä or "Purpurea Pendula'), invite one to an ideal sitting place.

The vine trellises of a bower can focus the view on house or garden like a *Passepartout*.

Under the wealth of rambling rose blossoms, even a simple wooden lattice structure becomes a romantically fragrant canopy.

Tucked away in the lap of nature, one can sit in this oval bower of woven willow withes. If one uses specially prepared withes of *Salix viminalis* or *Salix alba* and sticks them up to 15in. deep in the ground, they can take root and produce fresh greenery aboveground. Then the woven structure gradually disappears under the mantle of leaves. Whoever wants to can also train such a thick arboreal weave into desired shapes by trimming it, creating a jewel in a natural garden.

Rustic Bowers

They fit nicely into natural and country gardens and are usually made of wood. Living or non-living hazel or willow withes can also be woven artistically, and living ones will grow green in time and create a thick mantle.

While climbing supports of dowels or laths look very massive, finely worked trellises and pergolas can appear either more elegant or playful. To give a wooden bower a long life, stability, and sturdiness, one should use pressure-treated parts, especially softwoods, and anchor the supporting posts (at least 4in. diameter) firmly in the ground. So that the wind will not topple them, or unevenly heavy plant-growth tip them, screw the posts firmly to post anchors set 20-30in. deep into foundations. It is simplest to select concrete pipes with 8in. diameter, which can be filled with fresh concrete. In sheltered places, a simpler mounting in metal shoes with their long points driven into the ground will suffice while one inserts the posts above and screws them in. Note: If wooden bowers are to have a long life they should have no direct contact with the ground.

Massive round timbers form a tent-like, open-air domicile, loosely enlivened by climbing Clematis and hops, and inviting adventurous children to play Indians.

Such alcoves are easy to build around a bench with trellis grids and pergola elements. They can also be bought complete and colored to taste with weather-resistant enamel.

Plant Name	Location	Blossoms	Height	Soil	Tip
Tara Vine *Actinida arguta*	sunny	white, fragrant, May to June	15-21ft. (5-7m)	porous, nutrient-rich	edible fruit from October
Chocolate Vine *Akebia quinata*	sunny to part shade	violet, fragrant, April to May	6-12ft. (2-4m)	porous, nutrient-rich	cover young, plant in winter
Dutchman's Pipe *Aristolochia macrophylla*	sunny to shady	unlikely June to July	18-30ft. (6-10m)	mildly moist	decorative but poisonous
Anemone Clematis *Clematis montana*	sunny to part shade	white, rose, May to June	12-24ft. (4-8m)	porous, damp	fast-growing, many flowers
Clematis Varieties *Clematis viticella* and large-flowered hybrids	sunny to part shade	white, rose, red, blue, lilac June to October	9-18ft. (3-6m)	porous, mildly moist	many flowers when pruned
Russian Vine *Fallopia baldschuanica*	sunny to shady	white, fragrant, July to October	24-45ft. (8-15m)	sufficiently moist	grows fast, big, and heavy
Ivy (self-clinging) *Hedera helix* varieties	part shade to full shade	blooms only when old	15-60ft. (5-20m)	nutrient-rich, moist	needs no help, poisonous
Climbing Hydrangea *Hydrangea anomala ssp petiolar*	part shade to full shade	white, fragrant, June to July	15-21ft. (5-7 m)	mildly moist	fine yellow autumn color
Honeysuckle *Lonicera* varieties	sunny to shady	white, yellow, red, fragrant, May to August	9-15 ft. (3-5m)	porous, moist	fruit from August, poisonous
Woodbine (self-clinging) *Parthenocissus quinquefolia* *var. engelmannii*	sunny to part shade	unlikely, June	24-36ft. (8-12m)	porous, slightly moist	bright red autumn color
Rambling & Climbing Roses *Rosa* varieties	sunny to part shade	white, yellow, rose, fragrant, May to October	6-18ft. (2-6m)	deep, limed, moist	don't plant too closely
Thornless Blackberry *Rubus fruticosus* **types**	sunny	white, rose, May to August	9-18ft. (3-6m)	porous, moist	edible fruit from August
Wine Grapes *Vitis vinifera* **(many types)**	sunny	unlikely, May to June	18-30ft. (6-10m)	deep, limed	edible fruit from September
Crimson Glory Vine *Vitis coignetiae*	sunny to part shade	unlikely June to July	18-45ft. (6-15m)	porous	rust-red autumn color
Wisteria Varieties *Wisteria* **hybrids**	sunny to part shade	violet, white, fragrant April to May	18-30 ft. (6-10 m)	mildly moist	yellow autumn color, poisonous

Large bowers with massive posts and beams playfully bear the great weight of Wisteria.

Arabesques from the Plant World

Just as one plans the style, material, size, and shape of a bower creatively, one should also consider how it turns green, especially if one selects long-lived, often extremely heavy, husky climbing shrubs. Plants have an inherent style-setting power of expression. Lovely-leaved plants like Dutchman's Pipe spread attractive elegance, while the tender leaf-sea of Clematis, Roses, and Honeysuckle exude a playful and romantic magic, unlike grapevines, which exude a sensory bucolic flair.

Considerations in Choosing Plants

—**Whoever has children or pets should avoid poisonous plants.**

—**Choose types of climbing roses that are not overly thorny.**

—**Architectonically charming designs should not be completely overgrown by strong climbing vines.**

—**Even self-clinging vines should be tied at first, since they have a hard time gripping trellises.**

While climbing shrubs paint a picture that stays constant throughout the year, one can create a new outfit for the bower every year with annual climbers, whether with nostalgic Sweet Peas (*Lathyrus odoratus*), or green-and-white Japanese Hops (*Humulus japonicus* 'Variegatus').

Since many climbing plants, like Clematis, Roses, and others, tend to grow bald in their lower regions, it is recommended that these areas be brightened with medium to high-stemmed plants in front of them, such as fragrant bed roses, lilies, shrubs, decorative boxwood shapes – or with nicely arranged potted plants.

This shell-shaped half-round bower made of steel pipes is easy to assemble. The bower's thick green coat of Clematis almost conceals the supportive frame and gives it the character of a secret grotto.

Bower Nostalgia

Metal bowers look especially airy and filigreed, allowing the cheeriest flights of fancy. Whether based on historic patterns in wrought or cast iron, strap or round steel, or layered pipe in strict modern designs of aluminum or rusty Corten steel, many of these bowers are in no way inferior to pavilions in their artistic and elaborate roof designs. In the trade they are often called pavilions. With their lordly and airy construction, these small structures, also called gazebos, bring magic and atmosphere into the garden, which they enrich with an eye-catcher and divide as an element of height. If they are in visual contact with the house, their style should go with it. In an out-of-the-way area they can become surprising elements playing with fantastic visual effects.

The nobler their pattern, the more garlands of plants should play with them rather than hide them. For such merry capriccio, climbing roses (climbers, not bushy ramblers) and Clematis hybrids are especially suited, particularly the varieties of *Clematis viticella* with their somewhat smaller blossoms and resistance to usual Clematis wilting.

The color also defines the positional value of these airy refuges. While black, dark brown, and green let them blend in nicely, white, blue, red, and rust make them stand out clearly in a garden.

This magical sitting place is reminiscent of a private temple of the muses, with its paved circle matching the shape of bower and roof. A splendid example of the power of suggestion of a protected open space.

Garden centers and builders' markets meet the boom in the popularity of bowers and pavilions with models like these, which can be assembled easily as a do-it-yourself project.

Pavilions – Impressive Small-Scale Architecture

This pavilion, a precisely detailed reproduction, presents a charming example of the refined artistry of *art nouveau*. It forms a small realm of dreams for nostalgic contemporaries.

Although pavilions, like bowers, usually have open or half-open sidewalls, they differ from bowers by having a closed, usually very elaborate and decorative roof. No matter whether the shape is round, square, rectangular, pentagonal, or octagonal, they always offer room for several people in a very well-kept, though not always refined, style. This goes back to an almost four-thousand-year-old tradition of decorative structures, whether for the cult of the tea ceremony in Japan, a home for the muses in ancient times, or a manifestation of ruling power as in the Renaissance. Under the Rococo influence, pavilions grew grotesquely in the landscape gardens of the 18th century though all the romanticism and new experiences of the time were put into their conception. Thus they grew as reinvented antique, Gothic, Palladian, or Moorish temples, pagodas in pseudo-Chinese style or Turkish tents, straw-thatched hermitages or grottoes adorned with seashells. The furnishing fashions of the times can be followed easily in garden houses.

Today, mongrel forms are often described as pavilions when they bear fantastic or artistic roofs, like bowers with open but masterfully crafted roofs, or summer and garden houses with solid sidewalls and pavilion-like roofs. These are used as social sitting places, and they are also considered for storage of garden tools and utensils.

On the basis of their impressive and ornamental character, pavilions always need a certain field of open space around them. Thus, unlike bowers, they are not suited for tiny gardens. For all other gardens there are many of them available, made of wood, metal, plastic, steel pipe, and glass, in a wide variety of styles, colors, and price ranges.

This modern hexagonal pavilion made of galvanized iron stands out through its fine details. Its windows of cathedral glass are framed with satin glass and blue Goethe glass and can be opened in two sections.

Aspects of Planning

Whoever wants a pavilion in the garden should start by checking with the local authorities, for official permission may be required depending on the state and the means of construction. If the structure is to be located at the edge of the garden, there may be regulations as to its distance from the property line to keep in mind. In any case, it is a good idea to check with the neighbors and get their written permission.

Pavilions are usually heavier than bowers and thus require a particularly solid foundation. Depending on the model, this can be a spot foundation under the load-bearing pillars, a concrete slab, or an attractive paved or plate surface, which should usually take the same shape as the pavilion. If it extends beyond this, it offers more space for seating, for potted flowers, or for an outdoor grill. The size of this foundation itself can achieve very different effects. If it is very extensive, it can form a horizontal counterpoint to a vertical pavilion in the green of the garden and even influence its effect. A barely larger foundation, on the other hand, allows plantings – whether climbing vines, shrubs, or flowers – to come up to the building and thus integrate it artistically with the realm of plants.

The style, size, and structure of the pavilion should be considered carefully. Half-open or open sidewalls offer a panoramic view, as do closed models with windows, glass fronts, or doors with windows, which also offer protection from wind, dampness, and cold. Medallion-styled or artistically decorative window openings form frames that lead the gaze gently into the garden.

Electric connections should also be planned from the start. Even when one would rather spend summer evenings in romantic candlelight, outer illumination of the pavilion in the dark can have a fairytale effect.

This metal pavilion, with its columns and rich decoration, is reminiscent of a temple. Its eight angles make it appear almost round.

A Firm Foundation

—Excavate the planned surface 1 ft. deep.
—Put in rough fill 8 in. deep and compact it.
—Over it spread 2 in. of gravel or fine crushed stone and compact it.
—Over this spread 2 in. of sand or fine gravel.
—Over this lay paving stones or slabs. This foundation is sufficient for metal structures.
—For wooden structures, lay square hardwood timbers and build the pavilion on top of them. Thus air can circulate, avoiding the growth of fungus and mold.

This gigantic wooden deck, including sitting and lounging furniture and a nostalgic pavilion within its circular border forms a comfortable rest area by a pond. The pavilion combines the feeling of times gone by with modern ambience. The design shows courage in forming an unusual contrast of small and large surfaces, simple modernity, and lively ornamentation.

Like a scene from a romantic poem, this octagonal pavilion has settled in the midst of a garden and offers a new view of the colorful world of plants from every window.

Summery white defines this teahouse inside and out. Its light color brightens the deep shadows under the tall, old trees.

This hexagonal pavilion with its classic pagoda roof of copper and large, multi-paned windows contains an elegant eating place in white and gold.

Models Reflect the Times

Pavilions have always been high-class refuges and artistic eye-catchers, often in exotic international and fantastic styles. Whether richly ornamented pagodas or simply styled teahouses, the borders between styles and concepts tend to blur.

Today there are many forms and types available in wood, metal, glass, and combinations of them, in the most varied price ranges. Even builders' markets carry complete kits for the do-it-yourself builder. The specialist firms, on the other hand, offer more striking models.

Pavilions are decorations for the garden and thrive on fine details. Their roofs can be bell- or pagoda-shaped, pointed, cupola-like, curved, or stepped in many ways. Usually they are made of high-quality materials with one or more decorative edges. On half-open pavilions one often finds filigreed and ornamental vine trellises with round windows or vine-like decorations on the pillars. Closed ones often have a floor of fine parquet or luxurious tiles. The ribbed inner structures of the hexagonal and octagonal roofs are also decorative and can be painted to go with the interior. Artistic glazing, along with door and window handles complete the repertoire of the pavilions, which use their design and allure to promise a life of luxury in the world of nature.

The South Seas style of this pavilion, located idyllically under the umbrella of a tall tree, invites one to enjoy desert-island adventures.

The umbrella design, chiefly built of natural materials like bamboo and wood, offers refined simplicity.

Impressive Style in the Garden

Every garden has its strengths and weaknesses, which can be utilized or improved on by a pavilion. When you choose such a decorative structure, one should remember above all that the proportions of garden and garden residence should be balanced. A too-small pavilion disappears in a large area, while a too-large one can overwhelm a small space.

Finding the right place for a pavilion in a garden will require an individual decision in every case. But five typical garden situations can be examined to see how these little pleasure palaces have conjured up an emotional and joyful scenario for hundreds of years.

—They can lend a pleasant sparkle to a distant corner of a garden, and show house and garden from a hitherto unknown perspective. By using an unoccupied corner the garden appears larger, because it presents expressive and animating elements to the eyes and senses.

—Pavilions create unique garden scenes when they stand at the edge of a garden or a lawn under tall, old trees. The symbiosis of human work and nature is expressed here in splendid, intermingling when a mighty roof of leaves extends over the noble garden house like a sheltering umbrella.

—Pavilions afford ponds classic focal points by forming picturesque eye-catchers. At the same time, they let the magic of water, with its glittering surface in which light and season are reflected, be enjoyed dreamily from nearby. For this reason, pavilions were built on dredged-up islands or on Chinese bridges over the water in the new landscape gardens of the 18th century.

—Pavilions located on high spots, knolls, or slopes should always be designed stylishly with a refined sensibility. They catch the eye in a special way. The situation at hand should definitely be utilized and not distorted with shrubbery, since one can usually enjoy a beautiful view from above. Here too, we go back to the tradition of English landscape gardens of the 18th century with their artificial hills crowned by a temple of pavilion, as well as their belvederes – those partly artistic, partly grotesque bowers or pavilions whose elevated positions promised splendid views.

With gigantic front windows, this extravagant garden house opens onto the water. Its solid construction and its own terrace make it a genuine second home.

The charming pavilion enriches the layout of the slope in this garden, offering the rest-seeker lovely views from airy heights.

—But pavilions from formal gardens should not be disregarded. There they can glitter as central meeting points over intersecting paths, represent the longed-for goal at the end of an aisle or path, or be integrated into garden and wall corners as sentry boxes.

In contemporary formal gardens, pavilions always look enchanting when a path lined with boxwood leads straight to them and they are symmetrically adorned with geometric designs on both sides of the door. Among the magical possibilities are long-stemmed roses, boxwood spheres or spires, modern high conical containers with plants flowing down, nostalgic columns with stone ornaments or flower bowls, vine pyramids or obelisks on which climbing plants can unfold their splendor.

The best classic styling is seen in this garden layout with a square pavilion as crown and hideaway on the path that leads to it as a central axis.

From the pavilion in a formal garden one can see the geometric paths, their patterned effect strengthened by uniform plantings along their edges.

At the base of this fine design, Dwarf Periwinkle (*Vinca minor*) and Lady's Mantle (*Alchemilla mollis*) can spread out freely.

This pavilion with its double wing doors offers passage rather than a place to stay. The symbol of Hidcote Manor was charmingly designed like a theater box that signifies every scene as a high point.

Contributors

Garden Architects:

Ambiente Gartengestaltung Stender GmbH & Co., Münster
Architekturbüro Landschaft und Garten, Solingen
Helmut Boese – Vetter, BSL, Kassel
Bildhauerei Borhmann und Roth, Gredenstein
Florus Gartenbetrieb GmbH, Isernhagen
Monika Geissler, Landschaftsarchitektin, Gütersloh
Dorothea Haag, Gartenarchitektin, Langenhagen
B. Hammerich, Gartenarchitektin, Neustadt
Garten Helmert
Uwe Höcker
Peter Hübotter, Architekt, Hannover
Cornelia Issmer-Pfromm, Architektin BDA, Kassel
Uwe Isterling, Isterling und Partner, Hamburg
Heike Johanna Jahns, Avantgardeners, Bremen
Dipl.-Ing. Rainer Kaczor, KRL-Die Gartengestalter, Gredenstein
Anja Kracht, Lemgo
Kreikenbaum
Regula Ohlmeier, Kassel
Rheims + Partner, Landschaftsarchitekten, Krefeld
Horst Schümelfelder, Landschaftsarchitekt, Düsseldorf
Stey und Theiss
Hedwig Thol
Astrid Waltenberg, LICHT BLICK, Kassel
Christian Wegener, Hamburg

Garden Furniture and Accessories:

Country Garden
Versand für Garten- und Wohnkultur
Christa Plasa
Nagolder Strasse 27
72119 Ammerbuch-Pfäffingen
telephone 0 70 73/23 72. www.country-garden.de

Die Gartengalerie
Monika Tittlbach
Wössinger Strasse 15
75045 Walzbachtal-Wössingen
telephone 0 72 03/18 05
www.diegartengalerie.de

Garpa
Kiehnwiese 1
21039 Escheburg
telephone 0 41 52/92 52 00

Teak & Garden
Lübecker Strasse
46485 Wesel
telephone 02 81/9 62 66 11
www.teakversand.de

Weishäupl
83071 Stephanskirchen
telephone 0 80 36/90 68-0
www.weishaeupl.de

Renate Weber
Exklusive Architektur- und Gartenornamente aus England
Liszthof 10
49076 Osnabrück
telephone 05 41/6 51 27
www.renate-weber.de

Pavilions and Tea Houses:

Wolfgang Matt
Ländelstrasse 34
74382 Neckarwestheim
telephone 0 71 33/1 54

Udo Noller
Gartenstrasse 5
74427 Fichtenberg
telephone 0 79 71/2 22 66

Macarel
Seltersweg 55 a
35930 Giessen
telephone 06 41/9 75 89 21

More Schiffer Titles

www.schifferbooks.com

Pools, Patios, and Fabulous Outdoor Living Spaces: Luxury by Master Pool Builders. Tina Skinner & Melissa Cardona. You don't have to travel beyond the backyard to experience pure luxury. This book will show you how to transform your lawn into a personal paradise. Over 400 beautiful color photographs of spectacular backyard environments feature pools, spas, and fountains. More than just water features, you'll find a wide breadth of projects that inspire and amaze. Indulge your senses with exciting ideas in backyard design, intended to pamper and please even the pickiest home owners. Realize the potential of your backyard with the power of simple landscaping, elaborate poolside structures, waterfalls, fireplaces, and more. Transform your lawn into a lavish retreat, bound to make a huge splash with friends, family, and neighbors.
Size: 11" x 8 1/2" • over 410 color photos • 256 pp.
ISBN: 0-7643-1994-9 • hard cover • $49.95

Pure Deck-adence: A Guide to Beautiful Decks. Tina Skinner. Pure Deck-adence: A Guide to Beautiful Decks is a fantasy collection of real-life deck photos from all over the United States. From the humblest of condo balcony walkouts to the most elaborate sprawling wood structures, Pure Deck-adence explores the many possibilities of add-on outdoor home improvements. This pictorial essay explores America's fascination with outdoor living, from barbecue-centered constructions to the new immersion in hot tub culture. More than 240 full-color photographs provide a rich resource of ideas for those who dream of expanding their homes, and their horizons, with wood decks.
Size: 8 1/2" x 11" • 246 color photos • 160 pp.
ISBN: 0-7643-0445-3 • hard cover • $29.95

Garden Projects for the Backyard Carpenter. Tina Skinner. Here are enough projects to keep even the most productive do-it-yourselfer occupied through several seasons of warm weather. This book contains over 30 projects and ideas for ways to expand your living space outdoors. Beautiful color pictures illustrate many of the projects, and more than 130 illustrations and step-by-step instructions make it easy to create these backyard treasures. With this book you can make decks, shade shelters, gazebos, work and storage areas, decorative arbors, planter boxes, garden borders, comfortable benches, a

OTHER SCHIFFER TITLES

swing, a picnic table, doghouses, and a bluebird nesting box.
Size: 8 1/2" x 11" • 438 photos • 112 pp.
ISBN: 0-7643-1234-0 • soft cover • $19.95

Fancy Fences & Gates: Great Ideas for Backyard Carpenters. Tina Skinner. This inspiring compendium of beautifully designed and crafted fences and gates will inspire homeowners and handymen to get right to work. This is a rich resource of dozens of beautifully crafted fences, any one of which could be the envy of your neighborhood. A how-to section helps you plan, plot, and execute a fence project. Included are ideas for privacy fences, fence/planter combinations, built-in seating, and arbor gates. Styles represented include fences influenced by the Arts & Crafts movement and Asian and traditional European designs. There are great ideas for providing privacy for a deck, patio, pool, or hot tub, and great gates to frame impressive entryways.
Size: 8 1/2" x 11" • 74 photos, 12 graphics • 64 pp.
ISBN: 0-7643-1417-3 • soft cover • $19.95

Retaining Walls: A Building Guide and Design Gallery. National Concrete Masonry Association. Tina Skinner. Whether it's a challenging hillside, an uneven backyard, or a shrubless plot in need of planters, this book will provide nformation to solve any landscaping dilemma while adding curb appeal and value to your property. The National Concrete Masonry Association presents the essential guide to constructing segmental retaining walls with detailed, easy-to-follow diagrams and charts for do-it-yourself homeowners and landscape contractors alike. From the fundamentals to the latest research and modern techniques in segmental retaining wall construction, this colorful and inspiring gallery of design suggestions accompanies the expertly written step-by-step guide, and offers a plethora of landscaping ideas The exciting and attractive colors, textures, and styles of segmental retaining wall units available will inspire great new designs for all landscape styles.
Size: 8 1/2" x 11" • 136 color photos, 22 b/w diagrams • 128 pp.
ISBN: 0-7643-1836-5 • soft cover • $24.95

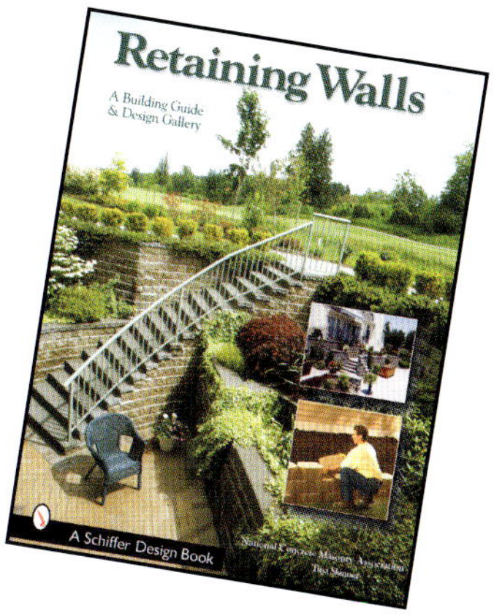

Schiffer books may be ordered from your local bookstore, or they may be ordered directly from the publisher by writing to:
Schiffer Publishing, Ltd.
4880 Lower Valley Rd
Atglen PA 19310
(610) 593-1777; Fax (610) 593-2002
E-mail: Info@schifferbooks.com

Please visit our web site catalog at ***www.schifferbooks.com*** or write for a free catalog.
Please include $3.95 for shipping and handling for the first two books and $1.00 for each additional book. Free shipping for orders $100 or more.

Printed in China

About the Authors

Gisela Keil comes from a family in which the joy of creating with gardens and plants has been fostered for generations. After studying German, English, and Comparative Literature, she has combined her love for books and gardens into a profession. For more than fifteen years she has been known as an author of garden books. As a gardening journalist, she also writes regularly for leading garden and lifestyle magazines.

Nik Barlo, Jr. has studied free art and visual communication. His garden and landscape themed photographs have been published in numerous displays, magazines, and books. He lives in Grebenstein, in northern Hessen, Germany.